A
HEART
OF
HOLINESS

In the late '70s, holiness became a hot topic. Preachers were preaching about it, and writers were writing about it. Then it seems the church moved on. But should we ever move on from something so central to the nature of God? I thank God that Daniel Seabaugh has gone countercultural on us. He tells us things every Christian should know—important, foundational material. My hope for the readers of this book is that holiness becomes core to their Christian identity and takes greater prominence in their lives as they join the unending hymn before the throne, "Holy, holy, holy is the Lord God, Almighty!"

Ron Watts, senior and founding pastor at La Croix Church in Cape Girardeau, Missouri

We're so accustomed to the media encouraging us to live for ourselves that the message becomes white noise. But that noise affects us in more ways than we realize. I'm thankful Daniel has written *A Heart of Holiness* to sing the song of wisdom, a song more biblical and beautiful than the banality of self. Make sure you read to the end of the book, because I found the last chapters on aging and death particularly challenging and encouraging. I'm sure others will, too.

Benjamin Vrbicek, lead pastor at Community Evangelical Free Church in Harrisburg, Pennsylvania, managing editor for Gospel-Centered Discipleship, and author of several books

What does it mean to live a holy life? Daniel Seabaugh has given us a wholistic primer on the Christian life. Accessible to believers of all ages and stages, *A Heart of Holiness* keeps the gospel central, exalts Christ, and turns our hearts to Scripture again and again.

> **Glenna Marshall**, author of *The Promise is His Presence*, *Everyday Faithfulness*, and *Memorizing Scripture*

If there were ever a time when Christians needed clear, biblical, grace-saturated teaching on what it means to live a holy life, it is now. In these pages, Daniel Seabaugh has given us a great gift as he instructs us in what it means and looks like to humbly and joyfully walk in holiness before our holy God. I am confident you will be greatly helped and encouraged as you soak in the truth and wisdom found in this little book. I will be recommending *A Heart of Holiness* to people for years to come.

> **Mark Hallock**, pastor at Calvary Church in Englewood, Colorado

A HEART OF HOLINESS

Cultivating *Wisdom* in a World of *Self*

DANIEL SEABAUGH

HARP & LYRE

A Heart of Holiness
Copyright © 2024 by Daniel Seabaugh

Published by Harp and Lyre
Cape Girardeau, MO 63701

ISBN (paperback): 979-8-218-39934-4

All rights reserved. No part of this publication may be reproduced, stored in a retrieval system, or transmitted in any form by any means—electronic, mechanical, photocopy, recording, or otherwise—except for brief quotations in printed reviews, without the prior permission of the publisher.

All Scripture references, unless otherwise indicated, are taken from the Holy Bible, New International Version®, NIV®. Copyright ©1973, 1978, 1984, 2011 by Biblica, Inc.™ Used by permission of Zondervan. All rights reserved worldwide. www.zondervan.com The "NIV" and "New International Version" are trademarks registered in the United States Patent and Trademark Office by Biblica, Inc.™

Scripture references marked CSB are taken from the Christian Standard Bible®, Copyright © 2017 by Holman Bible Publishers. Used by permission. Christian Standard Bible® and CSB® are federally registered trademarks of Holman Bible Publishers.

Scripture references marked ESV are taken from The ESV® Bible (The Holy Bible, English Standard Version®), copyright © 2001 by Crossway, a publishing ministry of Good News Publishers. Used by permission. All rights reserved.

Cover Design and Typesetting by Collin Smith Creative

*To Jesus.
I'd be utterly lost without you.*

*And Rachel.
Your love, faith, and contagious smile keep me going.*

Parts of this work appeared, in various forms and to various degrees, at DanielSeabaugh.com.

TABLE OF CONTENTS

Introduction: The Journey Ahead 11

ONE: Be Content With What You Have 17

TWO: Stop Striving! 31

THREE: Humility and Valuing Others 45

FOUR: On Not Loving the World 57

FIVE: Hearing and Doing 73

SIX: We Need Gospel Reminders 89

SEVEN: We Can't Stay Young Forever 103

EIGHT: Remember That You Will Die 119

Epilogue: Pursuing Holiness in an Unholy World 133

Acknowledgements 137

Endnotes 139

INTRODUCTION
THE JOURNEY AHEAD

*It is our habit to live for ourselves and not for God.
When we become Christians, we do not drop all this
overnight. In fact, we will spend the rest of our lives
putting off these habits and putting on
habits of holiness.*

— *Jerry Bridges, The Pursuit of Holiness*

God says, "Be holy, because I am holy" (1 Peter 1:16). That's a lofty command in an age when the autonomous self is pursued relentlessly, almost religiously. We love being rugged individualists, masters of our fate, and captains of our souls.[1] We admire people who plow their own course and make an impression on the world. But God's call to holiness challenges everything about our Western individualism. It's not good advice or something we do if we feel like it. God, the maker of heaven and earth, the one who gives life to every living creature, calls Christians to live differently than the world around them.

WHAT THIS BOOK IS AND ISN'T

This book is about holiness. But don't think holiness means submitting to a set of rules. Dos and don'ts won't make us holy. They'll change us, to be sure, but the change will resemble something other than holiness. We'll either be puffed up—believing we're better than everyone else—or, when we fail to live up to our impossible standards, we'll develop a low view of ourselves, believing we're failures and beyond God's reach. Neither approach reflects God's heart for people. Thankfully, another option exists. We'll explore it throughout these pages.

Holiness means being set apart—separated from sin and evil. It involves living in countercultural ways, obeying the voice of God in Scripture, and following a different set of standards than the world around us. More than anything else, holiness produces joy in us, promotes peace through us, and culminates in a God-glorifying, Spirit-empowered life. We must pursue it because, without holiness, no one will see God (Hebrews 12:14).[2]

This book isn't only about holiness, though. It's also about the Bible. The two work together. We grow in holiness as we obey the Holy Bible.

God exercises his authority through the pages of Scripture.[3] We can't celebrate the parts we like and throw away those we don't. We must obey every word.

> *All Scripture is God-breathed and is useful for teaching, rebuking, correcting and training in righteousness, so that the servant of God may be thoroughly equipped for every good work.*
>
> *—2 Timothy 3:16-17*

Kevin DeYoung says, "You can't make sense of the Bible without understanding that God is holy and that this holy God is intent on making a holy people to live with him forever in a holy heaven."[4] Holiness is all over the Bible.

The Bible should be lived, not just known. Putting its words into practice is far better than knowing a lot of its words. Perhaps you've met people who talk a lot about the Bible but live as if it's untrue or irrelevant. I don't want to live that way. I want to wholeheartedly follow Jesus, the crucified Christ, not an Americanized version of him.[5] Since you're reading this book, I'm guessing you do as well. I hope these pages serve you well.

At its core, *A Heart of Holiness* is about doing what the Bible says. I hope to inspire you to live the story of Scripture and experience its power. I want to help you cultivate wisdom through a time-tested method: reading God's Word and doing something about it.[6]

FORMING NEW HABITS

Before moving on, we should talk about habits. Since part of this book's aim is to develop holy habits in its readers, it's necessary to discuss them now.

We should question claims about transformation when they're paired with words like *easy, fast, overnight,* or some variation of these terms. Nothing worth doing happens in a day. It takes time and discipline to form new habits. It requires planning and intentionality. If we want to lose weight and keep it off, fad diets won't work. If we hope to retire at age fifty, we can't ignore our budget at forty. Learning to read and obey Scripture is no different.

Habits begin in the mind. Scripture says, "Be transformed by the renewing of your mind" (Romans 12:2), and "take captive every thought to make it obedient to Christ" (2 Corinthians 10:5). What we feed our minds is important because our actions flow from our thought lives. For example, if we fixate on negative words spoken to us, we'll likely become angry, bitter, or insecure. If we judge others internally, we'll likely become judgmental in our external world. An unfaithful spouse was lax in his thought life prior to the physical action that violated his marital covenant.

It's also true of holiness. If we don't set our minds to it, praying the Spirit of God works in and through us, we'll never become holy. The pursuit of holiness is a lifelong, Spirit-filled journey.

ENEMIES OF HOLINESS

We need God's Spirit to walk in holiness. But it's also important to acknowledge that we have an enemy—three, to be exact. These enemies will try to derail everything about our walk with Christ. Christians have historically recognized them as the world, the flesh, and the devil.[7]

In Scripture, *the world* refers to an "evil system, organized under the dominion of Satan and not of God."[8] We'll look at this definition again in chapter 4, but it's worth mentioning now. The world doesn't like God or anyone who does. Fleeing from its influence proves difficult because it's all around us. Therefore, we need to learn how to live wisely while in close proximity.

Selfish desires reside in *the flesh*. When we're tempted to eat an extra slice of pizza, our flesh is talking. When we lust after another person's spouse or covet our neighbor's property, our flesh is at work. The flesh acts disruptively in moments of stress or exhaustion. We should pay attention to where we turn for relief when feeling overwhelmed. Many unholy actions, such as overeating, overindulging, greed, or mindless surfing of the internet, happen in our weakest moments.

Not all desires are bad, of course. God places good desires in people. But because sin entered the world, our desires are perverted. The flesh, therefore, includes desires bent against God's will.

The third enemy we encounter is *the devil*. As C. S. Lewis warned in the preface to his classic book, *The Screwtape Letters*, people fall into two errors when thinking about the devil.[9] One error is to have an unhealthy and excessive interest in him. Oftentimes, this error is present when engaging in "spookiness" culture such as Halloween, horror movies, or paranormal activities. The second error happens when people disbelieve in the devil's existence altogether. Out of sight, out of mind.

The devil and his demons exist. Their main objective is to steal, kill, and destroy our lives. They don't have our best interests in mind. Satan does not want us moving toward Jesus. He is a murderer and a liar (John 8:44). He "prowls around like a roaring lion looking for someone to devour" (1 Peter 5:8).

The world, the flesh, and the devil work overtime. Thankfully, we can resist them. But as the world pulls further away from God's heart, enticing us to do the same, we must learn to navigate as foreigners in a land that feels directionless. It isn't easy. But the path has been blazed before. Take heart. We can be holy.

THE WHO AND HOW

This book was written for those new to the Christian faith, or perhaps for those exploring it. If that's you, I pray you're guided along the narrow road (Matthew 7:13-14). However, even if you've walked with Christ for years, something here will speak to you. We all need reminders. I want to remind us of Christ's beauty and the joy of walking with him.

Holiness will happen in our lives as the Spirit empowers us to walk it out day-to-day. Only God's Spirit can transform a life. What's more exciting than having the same Spirit who raised Jesus from the dead living in us? If we align our lives with his, forsaking all other allegiances, we'll experience transformation.

Each chapter of this book begins with a Bible verse. I'll tell you how the verse has impacted me and try to encourage you to apply it in your own life through God's power and grace. If you approach these verses as a list of dos and don'ts, this book will do more harm than good. If, however, you embrace them and fully surrender to God's Spirit, your life will be transformed.

God's Word is powerful. It has miraculous ways of shaking things up in us, rearranging areas we thought were dead, and illuminating those we thought were hidden in darkness. Over time, as we read and apply it, we'll become people who look a lot like Jesus. If we continue living in Scripture-obedience, we'll one day hear those precious words, "Well done, good and faithful servant" (Matthew 25:23)! I hope that's your desire. The goal of this book is to guide you toward holiness. It's an exciting journey because God goes with us, and God, in all his glory, is our destination.

CHAPTER 1

BE CONTENT WITH WHAT YOU HAVE

Keep your lives free from the love of money and be content with what you have, because God has said, "Never will I leave you, never will I forsake you."

—*Hebrews 13:5*

One of my favorite activities as a child was watching TV commercials with my parents. I particularly liked the ones when team members from the Publisher's Clearing House showed up on someone's doorstep holding an enormous check in their hands. Do you know the ones I'm talking about? The team arrived unannounced, cameras in tow, to surprise the homeowners with lots of money. The entire thing was filmed like a reality TV show. People lost their minds as they were presented with huge checks and promised money every month for the rest of their lives. Who wouldn't be excited about that? What an amazing feeling it must be!

Our family would have welcomed a visit from PCH. I hesitate to say we were poor because anyone living in the West is doing well compared to most of the world's population.[10] However, we did live near the Mississippi River, which flooded often and caused great damage to the houses in our neighborhood. Because of the potential for flooding, home values stayed low, as did the morale of neighbors.

During the flood of 1993, when I was six years old, I remember helping (at least, I thought I was helping) my neighbors put sandbags around their homes, which did a poor job keeping water out. Mud from the river covered the streets, and busted sandbags added grittiness to an already ugly situation. After the onslaught of water, people rowed boats from their back porches to fish upon the mighty Mississippi, which had, conveniently or inconveniently (depending on your perspective), imposed itself into their lives.

We were fortunate to live in a house on a hill, which kept the water away. But I'll never forget the smell of fish and muddy water that plagued the air. Nor will I forget the scene of homes underwater and people undone by their inability to do anything about it.

Growing up in a poor neighborhood presents some unique scenarios. One morning, while eating breakfast, a cockroach fell from the ceiling like a skydiver and landed in my bowl of cereal. You couldn't walk through our house without encountering these intrusive insects. It wasn't until I grew up and spent time around more affluent people that I realized cockroaches in your cereal was an oddity reserved largely for those living in poor neighborhoods. Yes, a visit from strangers offering us money would have been much appreciated.

What about you? If I arrived at your doorstep and told you that all your living expenses, such as food, clothing, and shelter, were taken care of for the rest of your life and that you would never again have to worry about feeding the children, clothing them, or working a dead-end job to keep the lights on, how would you respond? Would you shout for joy? Would you give me a hug? Would you go on vacation? Would you feel a huge weight lifted from you knowing that regardless of economic downturns, floods, skydiving cockroaches, or other factors that threaten a person's livelihood, your needs were met, you were set for life, and things were going to be okay?

Ironically, one of the things we believe will give us security and happiness can also produce great harm. Money can be a blessing. Indeed, it should be! It can address many of the needs around us. If allocated correctly, money could solve some of the world's problems, such as hunger. Yet despite all the benefits, money has cursed many unsuspecting people; the misuse of it has created many of the world's woes.

GREED AND IDOLATRY

Greed is a major problem today. From politicians to banking executives, insurance companies to car salesmen, greed has a tight grip on people. But it's more noticeable in others than it is in ourselves. We're blind to our own greed. We eagerly embrace the narrative that money can provide us security and freedom, then set off on a journey to make as much as possible, ignoring the greed lurking in our own hearts. Some of us spend our lives pursuing money without realizing how detrimental it is to our well-being.

Fixating on money corrupts and enslaves us to a life of hustle. In the beginning, our desire is harmless, wanting to provide for our basic needs and the needs of those under our care, but in the end, our desire to make more and more consumes us. It's a trap I've seen many times.

A HEART OF HOLINESS

Consider parents. To provide for their family, many obsess over stacking cash and become nonexistent in the home. When a spouse or child confronts them, they become irritated, argumentative, and illogical. What starts as a caring act ends as a point of tension for many families.

Or consider business owners. To rise above competitors, many cut corners, disregard the poor working conditions of their employees, and make immoral decisions. They begin a ruthless pursuit of the dollar, stepping over anyone who hinders their success.

Greed arrives unannounced. It sneaks up on its victims to choke the life out of them. Timothy Keller says,

> Why can't anyone in the grip of greed see it? The counterfeit god of money uses powerful sociological and psychological dynamics. Everyone tends to live in a particular socioeconomic bracket. Once you are able to afford to live in a particular neighborhood, send your children to its schools, and participate in its social life, you will find yourself surrounded by quite a number of people who have more money than you. You don't compare yourself to the rest of the world, you compare yourself to those in your bracket. The human heart always wants to justify itself and this is one of the easiest ways. You say, "I don't live as well as him or her or them. My means are modest compared to theirs." You can reason and think like that no matter how lavishly you are living.[11]

Greed is sneaky. It deceives us and leads us down a path of comparison. We become frustrated—endlessly spinning our wheels for wealth while frowning upon the greedy people of the world, especially those who take our slice of the pie.

It's widely reported that John D. Rockefeller, one of the wealthiest men who ever lived, was once asked how much money is enough, to which he replied, "Just a little bit more." Whether the encounter happened or not, we all believe a little bit more money would improve our lives and make us happier. We strive, therefore, working ourselves to death and filling our time with activities that ultimately produce anxiety and stress, enemies of happiness. We overextend ourselves for the accumulation of "a little bit more."

Greed is a major problem, no doubt. It's a sin we must guard against (Luke 12:15). When we give ourselves over to the pursuit of money in a way that is ultimate and god-like, our appetite for more goes unquenched. In the long run, we wind up feeling lied to because money over-promises and under-delivers. Money can't provide us with security, happiness, or contentment.

Furthermore, apart from the work of the Holy Spirit in a person's heart, no one is truly neutral when it comes to their desire for money. Those without money believe life would be better with it. Those with money believe life would be better with a little more. Such a perspective makes contentment very difficult. Hebrews commands us to keep our lives free from the love of money for this precise reason.

Money doesn't only make us greedy, though; it can also lead to idolatry. I once worked with a girl who was very talented at singing and dancing. She'd share videos of her performances with our team from her various social media accounts. These videos made quite a splash online. A couple went viral. It surprised me to see how many followers she had, not because she wasn't talented; she certainly was, but because I didn't believe

A HEART OF HOLINESS

such things happened to people living in Southeast Missouri.

One day, I asked her what she hoped to accomplish with all the attention garnered online. She told me, "I'm going to be a world-famous influencer. Everyone will know my name. I'll travel the world. My performances will sell out. I'll have more money than I know what to do with."

I replied, "That's so cool! I hope this works out for you. I can tell you really love what you're doing." She nodded with enthusiasm.

"What are you going to do if it doesn't work out?" I asked, mostly out of curiosity. "Do you have something else in mind?"

She looked at me like I was speaking another language.

"Oh, it's going to work out," she exclaimed. I continued to press her.

"Yeah, I know you're hopeful. But what if it doesn't?" She did not let my questioning deter her one bit.

"This is my whole life, Daniel!"

No matter what I said, she wasn't going to let my questioning stop her from achieving stardom. She convinced herself that fame wasn't a matter of *if*, but *when*. As far as I know, she never became world-famous. In fact, I don't know where she is today.

For my friend, her desire for fame became an idol. She couldn't imagine a fulfilling life without it. We look to idols for significance, purpose, and meaning in life. We spend our energy investing in them. We become agitated when people criticize them. We assume anyone who speaks against them is against us.

One of the best ways to determine whether something has become an idol is to ask the question, "Would I still be happy if this thing were no longer in my life?" Jesus said, "Where your treasure is, there your heart will be also" (Matthew 6:21). If our happiness is dependent on something other than God, we have an idol.

Idols may provide happiness for a season, but if we live long enough, they will lose their ability to fulfill us. For instance, if youth and beauty are idols, we'll feel crushed by the reality of aging. If money is an idol, a serious economic downturn will fill us with fear and anxiety.

In the Old Testament, idols were worshiped often. They generally took the form of images made of wood, stone, or metal and were believed to embody pagan deities. These gods were called upon to bring about certain desirable results. Whether rain for crop production or fertility for life, people clung to their idols in hopes of receiving blessings. In the West, idols rarely look like statues or images but often take the form of status and self-image. We also seek blessings from our idols by believing they'll fulfill us and make us great if we give them proper attention.

God has always forbidden the worship of idols, regardless of their form. The first of the ten commandments says we shall have no other gods before him (Exodus 20:3). Even though our idols look different, they are just as destructive as those found in the Old Testament.

Here's a list of some common idols found in our world. It's far from an exhaustive list, but it will hopefully provide an idea of the vast range of idolatry. Notice how the items listed are mostly good things. Idolatry usually takes good things and turns them into ultimate things.

• Money • Sex • Career • Youth • Beauty • Power • Ethnicity • Political Affiliation	• Marriage • Ideology • Parenting • Retirement • Inheritance • Hobbies • Nature • Education	• Religion • Comfort • Approval • Success • Art • Sports • Autonomy • Status Symbols

These idols, and a whole slew of others, vie for our attention. We give our lives to them because of their harmless appearance and delightful claims. Yet as God's dearly loved children, we must keep ourselves from idols (1 John 5:21).

SEEKING PERFECTION

Have you ever felt frustrated by the lack of perfection in our world? Perhaps you've spent time researching a product, seeking advice, and learning the ins and outs so as to make an informed buying decision, only to discover blemishes or imperfections upon purchase. We often turn to idols because we're looking for perfection. Even if our coveted item seems perfect, it's only a matter of time before it becomes outdated or suffers wear and tear. Nothing is perfect, and nothing lasts forever. I've learned that lesson on more than one occasion.

Recently, one of my daughters made me a Father's Day card, which was both impressive and hilarious. It was impressive because she's a talented artist, adding intricate details to drawings that make each one special, and it was hilarious because she took three of my favorite things and drew me doing all of them at once. If only I could ride my bicycle while drinking coffee and reading a book, I'd believe I had died and gone to heaven.

Riding my bicycle is a joy. I spent years riding and researching bikes before buying the one I now own. The color is perfect. It's called Chlorine Dream, which is the best blue in existence. I purchased the bike during the pandemic of 2020 and 2021, when it was next to impossible to find bicycles. The two shops in my hometown said, "We can't get it. If you find one, you should probably buy it." I called every bike shop within a 200-mile radius and managed to locate one in Nashville, TN. My wife and I made the trip, spent an evening in a hotel, found a great coffee spot, and bought a bicycle.

Once we got the bike home, I discovered a scratch in the paint—yes, the paint I loved was flawed. Nothing is perfect on this side of heaven. Everything gets scraped, tattered, worn, and bruised. It's part of the fall and curse of humanity. We seek perfection, but it's always out of reach.

Let me share another story. I love buying Bibles. In my mind, having access to multiple translations is a good thing. After convincing my wife that owning another Bible was a good idea, I bought one online with a goatskin leather cover. Once the Bible arrived, I noticed the printing along the spine was off-center. The translation logo was printed too far to the right and the publisher's name too far to the left. Again, not perfect.

Did I return the Bible, get my money back, or leave a bad review online? No. Part of growing in holiness is learning that nothing in life is perfect. Every time I pick up my Bible or ride my bicycle, I'm reminded of that truth. Even if we spend top dollar on something, it won't last forever. Our search for perfection isn't met in this life.

Yet our verse in Hebrews, cited at the start of this chapter, suggests one thing that lasts forever—something we should seek in this life, something of absolute perfection, something we can never lose.

WHAT WE CAN NEVER LOSE

I began this chapter by asking what your response would be if I showed up on your doorstep and offered you enough money to sustain you for the rest of your life. Because there is so much uncertainty in life, I wanted you to consider the emotions you'd feel if I offered something certain, something you couldn't lose.

The writer of Hebrews knew we'd turn to money for contentment. That's why we're commanded to keep our lives free from the love of it. The love of money leads us away from true contentment—a peace that sustains us all our days. The Apostle Paul, who encountered the risen Jesus in a powerful way, learned the secret to being content in any and all circumstances (Philippians 4:11-12). Furthermore, while writing to his coworker, Timothy, Paul shared some amazing insights about contentment.

> *But godliness with contentment is great gain, for we brought nothing into the world, and we cannot take anything out of the world. But if we have food and clothing, with these we will be content. But those who desire to be rich fall into temptation, into a snare, into many senseless and harmful desires that plunge people into ruin and destruction. For the love of money is a root of all kinds of evils. It is through this craving that some have wandered away from the faith and pierced themselves with many pangs.*
>
> *— 1 Timothy 6:6-10 ESV*

BE CONTENT WITH WHAT YOU HAVE

And just to make sure people were clear that having money is not a problem, but only attaching our hearts to it, Paul gave instructions to the rich people under Timothy's care.

> *Command those who are rich in this present world not to be arrogant nor to put their hope in wealth, which is so uncertain, but to put their hope in God, who richly provides us with everything for our enjoyment. Command them to do good, to be rich in good deeds, and to be generous and willing to share. In this way they will lay up treasure for themselves as a firm foundation for the coming age, so that they may take hold of the life that is truly life.*
>
> —*1 Timothy 6:17-19*

Paul understood that money is unable to provide contentment. Only Jesus can fulfill us. We're created to know him, love him, and glorify him with our lives. The appetite raging within us is only satisfied in Christ.

Jim Elliot, an American missionary who lost his life trying to reach the Huaorani Indians of Ecuador, wrote in his journal that "he is no fool who gives what he cannot keep to gain what he cannot lose." When the book of Hebrews says to be content with what we have, it's claiming that contentment is found in God's presence, not God's presents.

God lavishes us with many good, material gifts that should be enjoyed in this life. But material blessings are not where we find contentment. If we fixate on them, we'll simply love the good gifts God gives, not the God who gives good gifts. God's presents should never replace God's presence as the source of our contentment. If we belong to Christ, God's presence is the one thing we'll never lose. It's a promise.

Bob Marley said, "Money can't buy life." No amount of money will make us happy. The Publisher's Clearing House can't satisfy the deep hunger found in every human heart.

Hebrews 13:5 is the sweetest promise: God will never leave us or forsake us. The possessions we seek won't last; the money we invest could be gone tomorrow; and the house we renovate could catch fire. Only God's love, given ultimately at the cross, will last forever. Because he died, taking the punishment we deserve because of our sin, we can live knowing that nothing can separate us from the love we have in Christ Jesus (Romans 8:38-39). We don't have to fear the future. We don't have to feel guilty about the past. We don't have to live today with something to prove to the world tomorrow.

God will never leave us or forsake us. What if we sin? God will never leave us or forsake us. What if our health fails? God will never leave us or forsake us. What if we lose our jobs? God will never leave us or forsake us. What if we suffer and he doesn't heal us? He will be with us in the suffering, for he has promised to never leave us or forsake us. What about the horrendous acts of evil done throughout the world? Where is God's presence in those moments? Because Jesus took the sins of the world upon himself, everything will be redeemed. All that is wrong will be made right. We have a hope that can never be taken from us. All who trust in the finished work of Jesus have a good future and a friend who stays closer than a brother (Proverbs 18:24).

God promises his presence. He'll never leave us. He'll never forsake us.

FINAL THOUGHTS ON CONTENTMENT

I'll never forget my wedding day. Because we love the mountains, Rachel and I decided to get married near the Great Smoky Mountain National Park. The ceremony happened in a small chapel. The guy who officiated smelled of cigarettes and booze. I'm pretty sure he was mowing the grass when we arrived at the venue. His disheveled appearance concerned us very little. He did his thing, then we headed to Starbucks for a latte before setting off on the Appalachian Trail. Our future was wide open, and we spoke about it with excitement. We dreamed of children, ministry, and life together.

Last year, we returned to the Smokies. We've been married for over a decade now, and God has taught us many things. During our recent visit, I jotted down some thoughts about contentment. I want to share them here before closing out this chapter.

God is the reason for our contentment. Him alone. When we understand that truth deeply and without reservation, we can look with gratitude at some of the gifts he has given.

1. *We must find contentment in what we already have, not in the things we believe will produce contentment once we have them.*

It's okay to enjoy God's presents. This may feel like a contradiction to everything we just discussed. It's not. If Christ is our hope, the one we find our contentment in, his gifts are blessings, nothing more. When our desires are fulfilled in Christ alone, we get his blessings thrown in. Many of us live with desires for material possessions or the fulfillment of dreams. Attaining goals is not wrong. I've accomplished many goals and am thankful for the time I invested in them. The problem lies with believing that reaching a dream or goal will provide contentment—or that God's gifts will. If we live with such a perspective, our lives will move from one frustration to the next. We'll always chase the next goal. We won't learn how to be content with what we have, like Hebrews 13:5 commands.

2. Contentment can be found in limitations.

Being a parent produces limitations for a couple, particularly in the early years. Before we had children, Rachel and I hiked strenuous mountains with amazing views. We went where we wanted when we wanted. We never imagined things would change. Now that we have young children, even small nature hikes prove challenging. We've learned there's joy in embracing our limitations. Our children's stage of life dictates our activities.

On our last mountain excursion, our children played in front of our cabin. Laughter filled the air instead of frustration. We traded our usual agenda of climbing mountain peaks and eating local cuisine for catching crawdads in the creek beside us. In this season, we embrace our limitations and find contentment in what we have.

Rachel and I have seen many of our dreams come to pass, and many go to be with the Lord. Though we haven't won every battle, God has taught us that he's our greatest treasure. He'll never leave us or forsake us. God is the reason for our contentment. His presence and power are the greatest blessings of all.

CHAPTER 2

STOP STRIVING!

"Be still, and know that I am God; I will be exalted among the nations, I will be exalted in the earth."

— *Psalm 46:10*

Have you ever spent time in a big city? Like a really big city? The sights, sounds, and smells almost knock you over. It's like there's an energy or buzz hanging over the air—a unique noise permeating the atmosphere. Everything pulsates. Traffic screams. Subways roar. Cities never sleep.

I'm not a huge fan of cities. Perhaps it's because of my upbringing in a small town. In small towns, everyone knows your name and shops at the same grocery store. Sure, I enjoy visiting cities for brief stints, but I'm always anxious in the middle of all the activity. The clinking, clacking, drilling, honking, and rushing do something negative to my mental state.

I know people who experience the opposite. Cities bring them life in wonderful ways. Cities allow them to embrace the fullness of who God made them to be; they don't see obstacles in cities, only opportunities. Even God has a soft spot for cities.

> *But seek the welfare of the city where I have sent you into exile, and pray to the LORD on its behalf, for in its welfare you will find your welfare.*
>
> *— Jeremiah 29:7 ESV*
>
> *Instead, they were longing for a better country—a heavenly one. Therefore God is not ashamed to be called their God, for he has prepared a city for them.*
>
> *— Hebrews 11:16*

One upside to cities is the amenities. A person can find anything within a few blocks. Intriguing art? Check. The world's best cup of coffee? Done. Donuts that were baked on the moon? There's a bakery around the corner. Unlike small towns, cities offer options. You can get what you want, when you want it, and find something you didn't know you wanted in the process. Cities are great for that reason.

They're also exciting because of the culture they produce. Some of the most talented people in the world live in cities. Whether it's musicians, foodies, writers, or various creative types, cities beam with the artistic endeavors of their citizens. Cities are full of interesting people.

I once met a guy on a city street who could tell you your zip code if you told him where you were from. He was a local legend. Crowds gathered around him like he was a rock star.

But despite all the grandeur, cities don't always produce good things. Sometimes, the heart of a city has its foundation in wickedness. There's an account in the Bible where one of the first cities ever built greatly displeased God.

> *Now the whole world had one language and a common speech. As people moved eastward, they found a plain in Shinar and settled there. They said to each other, "Come, let's make bricks and bake them thoroughly." They used brick instead of stone, and tar for mortar. Then they said, "Come, let us build ourselves a city, with a tower that reaches to the heavens, so that we may make a name for ourselves; otherwise we will be scattered over the face of the whole earth. But the LORD came down to see the city and the tower the people were building. The LORD said, "If as one people speaking the same language they have begun to do this, then nothing they plan to do will be impossible for them. Come, let us go down and confuse their language so they will not understand each other." So the LORD scattered them from there over all the earth, and they stopped building the city.*
>
> — *Genesis 11:1-8*

Do you see what's going on here? These people wanted to build a city to make a name for themselves. They didn't care about God or his glory. The act of building was self-centered. They sought their own preservation, as seen in their comment, "otherwise we will be scattered over the face of the whole earth."

Cities can be like that even today—their architectural majesty like a sign screaming, "Look at us! Aren't we great?"[12] The planning and building of a city can be, in part, a way to create a heaven on earth, where health, wealth, joy, peace, and safety are experienced by all living in it. There's nothing wrong with any

A HEART OF HOLINESS

of that, per se, unless God is removed from the picture. The removal of God is precisely what's happening in the story above.

Notice how God responded. He thwarted the plans of these people. He was not pleased with their work. His actions were opposed to theirs. They sought to "go up" as it were, building a city reaching the heavens, but God "came down" not only to see the city and tower but to confuse their language and stop their work.

God wanted his people to fill the earth (Genesis 1:28; 9:1, 7), bear his image, and bless people everywhere they went. The people in this story, however, didn't care about God's will, mission, or their role in image-bearing. They were afraid of being scattered, so they built a city. Ironically, by building a city, they wound up being scattered. They overstepped their divinely ordained limits, trying to become like God.[13]

It's always tempting to look at historical events in the Bible and think, "What a bunch of ungrateful people! How could they possibly disregard God after everything he did for them?" We often assume if we lived in their time and were faced with their problems, we'd handle things differently. We'd listen to God, not turn to the right or left. But we're not immune to disobedience. Not by a long shot.

The Scriptures say God will not yield his glory to another (Isaiah 42:8). Regardless of our best efforts, God is not pleased with our work when he's removed from the equation. We must learn to be still, stop fighting, and cease striving so we can live our lives under the care and authority of King Jesus.

Being still isn't about sitting quietly before God like monks, though I suppose it can include that. Stillness exalts God, not self. Psalm 46:10 teaches us to trust God's provision, not our ability to conquer. It's about thinking of ourselves with sober judgment, not higher than we ought (Romans 12:3). It's about saying God is God and we are not. His name will be exalted above all other names.

MAKING A NAME FOR OURSELVES

From a very young age, we make life all about us. Think of a baby. Anyone who has raised a baby knows it's one of the best and hardest things in life. Babies are blessings from the Lord. But if parents don't train them in the way they should go, they'll become a pain in the neck to everyone around them (Proverbs 22:6). They'll continue crying to get their way, which is sort of cute when they're little and certainly not wrong, but entirely uncalled for at age thirty.

We fight to be heard. We long to be seen. The world trains us in the school of "prove yourself." Our society is a breeding ground for competition. We want to get our way and exalt ourselves.

Think of social media. It provides an opportunity for everyone to curate their lives so as to make a name for themselves. It's one of the reasons the internet has become what it is today. We all want to be significant. We want others to know who we are and what we're capable of. Pay no mind to the fact that social media is a facade, an illusion. People only post their highlight reels.

We're physical creatures, designed to live face-to-face with others, but the internet has taken large steps to connect us to a disconnected, disorienting cyberworld. People spend countless hours on social platforms portraying a life of significance. It's isolating and lonely. It's causing great harm. Depression is on the rise. So is mental health.[14] Humanity is suffering. Making a name for ourselves isn't working.

Or consider our ruthless attempts to climb the success ladder. The West has largely defined success by having large bank accounts, letters behind our names, overly priced vehicles, and nice homes in nice neighborhoods with great schools. Everyone competes to be the best and rise above the rest. When we live this way, the main objective of our lives becomes competition, proving our worth, and trying to add value to our existence. It never stops. We yearn for influence. We race to the top. Brick by brick, we build our cities, desperately searching for an identity.

OUR DESPERATE SEARCH FOR IDENTITY

We all do it. We derive our significance and self-worth from something or someone. It can be a career, a relationship, a hobby, or a cultural concept or idea. When we attempt to find self-worth in anything other than the one who created us, problems arise.

When I was studying at Denver Seminary, I became obsessed with Coloradan culture. There are many things to love about that state. There's a great bicycle scene; fresh and organic food options; all the coffee and experimental beverages a connoisseur could dream up; and a "be whoever you want" mentality that's refreshing.

I loved everything Colorado had to offer. One problem existed, however. I didn't just want to live the mountain culture; I wanted everyone I knew to associate me with such things. I never admitted it then, partially because of my deception and desperate search for an identity, but when I posted something online, I wanted everyone, especially my friends back home, to think my life was cooler than theirs because I lived in the mountains. I was determined to live the life I thought others wanted at the expense of living the life God wanted me to live. In short, Colorado was my identity. Yet those were some of my darkest days.

The Bible talks a great deal about finding identity *in Christ* or *in God*. The book of Ephesians is full of such phrases. It's a theme throughout much of the New Testament.

In what follows, I'll provide three statements I've repeated to myself over the years to fight against finding an identity in this world. I hope they encourage you to seek holiness in this area of your life.

1. You are not what you do.

The statement "you are what you do" is a lie from the pit of hell. And, sadly, our world believes it. One of the main questions I heard during college was a variation of "What are you studying?" and "What do you want to do when you graduate?" Some people were simply trying to have a friendly conversation, I'm sure. They weren't intending to ask questions related to identity. Yet others, whether they'd verbalize it or not, were measuring my worth and future success by my choice of degree.

If a person studies something related to medicine, the thought goes, they'll likely have a great life with many material and social blessings. On the other hand, if a person studies philosophy, like I did, they shouldn't get their hopes up for much reward. Lumping people into categories isn't encouraging or Christlike. And there is more to life than what we do.

Finding an identity in what we do will look different for everyone. For some, hard work is their identity. For others, it's found in voting Republican or Democrat. Like idolatry, the places from which we seek identity are vast.

We are not what we do. We belong to Christ. Our lives are hidden with him (Colossians 3:3). As Christians, we have a certain hope. Our future is gloriously fixed. It doesn't matter what college degree we choose or career we pursue so long as our hearts are set on things above, namely, on Christ, who is our life.

2. Your worth is not in what you own.

There's a beautiful hymn with a similar title written, no doubt, to help us center our hearts and minds around the truth that Christ is our greatest treasure. Like the statement "you are what you do," we often believe our worth comes from the amount of stuff we own or the zeros behind the numbers in our bank accounts.

The entire hymn contains lyrics full of gospel truths, but here are a few powerful lines reminding us to fixate on Christ, not material things:

> *As summer flow'rs we fade and die*
> *Fame, youth and beauty hurry by*
> *But life eternal calls to us*
> *At the cross*
>
> *I will not boast in wealth or might*
> *Or human wisdom's fleeting light*
> *But I will boast in knowing Christ*
> *At the cross*

The belief that our stuff makes us valuable makes me think about the bumper sticker that says, "Whoever dies with the most toys wins." It's not true, but droves of people buy it and squander their lives in the process.

3. Your circumstances do not define your value.

I don't know what your life currently looks like. You may feel marvelously blessed—better than you ever imagined possible. Praise God if so! But don't believe for a second your life is valuable because of your current situation.[15] Circumstances can change in an instant.

Let us remember what David wrote about the brevity of life in Psalm 39:4-5. He said our lives are fleeting and that we should learn to number our days. We'll pick up this theme more extensively later, but David says even those *who seem secure* are but a breath. Our sense of security today may set us up for sadness, grief, and despair tomorrow. We must turn to the one who finds us valuable—not because of what we do or what we own, not because of our current circumstances, but because he created us and loves us.

Our identity should be found in Christ alone. The cry of our hearts should be "I belong, entirely and eternally, to Jesus!" He's the only person who will satisfy our craving to be somebody special because, in him, we already are.

NO MORE FIGHTING

The Christian Standard Bible translates the often-quoted words "be still" from Psalm 46:10 as "stop fighting." As much as I like the former, I'm growing to appreciate the latter. God will make wars cease, as verse 9 tells us. Therefore, the words stop fighting are completely appropriate given the context of this Psalm.

Since the fall of humanity, God's people have fought with themselves and others. In some people's minds, the word *fighting* is synonymous with the word *church*. But as God's chosen people, set free by the gospel of Jesus, fighting to make a name for ourselves should not exist among us. After all, blessed are the peacemakers (Matthew 5:9). We're called to be a people of reconciliation. We're called to build others up, not tear them down to build our own cities or platforms.

A great deal of fighting today has to do with our attempts to build a city that specializes in self-exaltation. In our constant activity of making much of ourselves, we plow others down, treat them with disrespect, and push back anytime they try to encroach on our city. But at the end of all things, when this earth has run its course and the maker of heaven and earth comes to reclaim and redeem what's currently corrupted by sin, there will be a great city, in fulfillment of the promise God gave to Abram (whose name was later changed to Abraham) in the Old Testament.

> *The LORD said to Abram, "Go from your country, your people and your father's household to the land I will show you. "I will make you into a great nation, and I will bless you; I will make your name great, and you will be a blessing. I will bless those who bless you, and whoever curses you I will curse; and all people on earth will be blessed through you."*
>
> *— Genesis 12:1-3*

God's intention has always been to bless the nations of the world through the family lineage of Abraham. Isn't it interesting how God condemned the builders of the city and tower in Genesis 11 for attempting to make a name for themselves, yet he promised Abraham he'd make his name great? Do you see the difference between these two accounts? Abraham's blessing was bestowed on him by the God of Israel, the one true God.

The people in the tower account were seeking to establish their own reputation, apart from God or his blessing. Without God's intervention, all the work of our hands is done in vain.

> *Unless the LORD builds the house, the builders labor in vain. Unless the LORD watches over the city, the guards stand watch in vain.*
>
> *— Psalm 127:1*

Instead of striving to get our way, building our brand, reputation, or city, we must learn to rest in God. He's enough. We don't have to become someone of importance. We're already people of immeasurable worth to God. The life, death, resurrection, and ascension of Jesus prove our lives matter. We can cease striving. We don't have to prove ourselves to anyone any longer.

Being still—knowing that God is in control and being content with the fact that we aren't—will be a lifelong endeavor, no doubt. We'll have to learn to tune out the voices around us saying we must build a city. We'll have to break free of the comparison trap, the rat race. With that in mind, I can think of three ways to live today in stillness before God and others.

1. Celebrate the victories of others with no strings attached.

God's will is accomplished through the work of many saints. It takes a village. It's not about us. When peers accomplish great feats at work, we should celebrate it with them, not envy their success. We should rest in the fact that good work was done, not think of ways to outdo it, which, if we're honest, is about outdoing them and exalting ourselves. By celebrating the victories of others, our minds get off ourselves and onto Christ and his kingdom.

2. Seek to be a servant, not just to serve.

We shouldn't keep our talents to ourselves. If we have expertise in an area, we should share it with others, especially those who want to grow in that area. If a person knows how to navigate the financial world, she should share that knowledge with a young parent or somebody new to the workforce who's likely thinking about finances. If a man knows how to work on vehicles, he shouldn't simply start an automotive repair shop or think of ways to turn his knowledge into cash; he should teach someone else who cares about car repair how to do it, too. In the words of Jesus, "It is more blessed to give than to receive" (Acts 20:35).

When we give our gifts away instead of making them about us, we learn stillness—we stop trying to exalt ourselves. We can't simply seek to serve, though, as that keeps the control in our court. We must voluntarily become servants. There's a difference. Serving must be who we are, not simply what we do. When we become servants, we learn to be still, cease striving, and stop fighting.

3. Be willing to give your resources away.

Nothing truly belongs to us. We're called to be good stewards of the gifts God gives. If there's a need within our ability to meet, we should do so eagerly. What good is there in hoarding?

We should welcome opportunities to give our stuff away. If we cling to stuff, it'll cling to us, destroying our lives over time.

Like the early church, we should be willing to sell our things and give to those in need (Acts 2:45). Just as serving helps us be still, so does a willingness to give our resources away to those in need.[16]

Let me conclude with a meditation from St. Patrick using Psalm 46:10. Read it slowly. Consider placing your hands in front of you, palms down, which is the posture of loosening your grip. Imagine letting go of striving. No more fighting. No more making a name for yourself. Let God be exalted in your life. Picture your anxiety hitting the floor in front of you as you slowly read the following words:

Be still and know that I am God.

Be still and know that I am.

Be still and know.

Be still.

Be.

CHAPTER 3

HUMILITY AND VALUING OTHERS

*Do nothing out of selfish ambition or vain conceit.
Rather, in humility value others above yourselves.*

— *Philippians 2:3*

Perhaps you've heard the claim, "I'm so humble. It's one of my best traits." I'd hear claims like these when working in the marketplace and interviewing job candidates. The wording always struck me as odd. Surely anyone making such a claim lacks the character trait he wants you to believe he has. Yet, truthfully, I felt a bit like that person while writing this chapter.

Although it's the third chapter you're reading, it's the last one I'm writing. It's by far the hardest one to write. Humility is difficult to talk about because it disappears as soon as you begin. To think you're humble is a sure sign you're not.

C. S. Lewis claimed if we encountered a truly humble man, we'd likely not know it but merely notice the cheerfulness with which he lived. He certainly wouldn't go around thinking about humility, for he wouldn't be thinking about himself at all.[17] Identifying humble people, therefore, proves challenging. They're hidden in plain sight. Because it's difficult to identify them, ask them questions, or peer into their lifestyle choices, problems arise while trying to develop humility or write about the subject.

The Bible speaks about humility in positive ways. I once spent a couple months highlighting all the passages I could find about it. One of the interesting things I found was how the Bible contrasts humility with pride. Pride is the opposite of humility. Look at a few of the ways the Bible talks about the two:

Pride goes before destruction, a haughty spirit before a fall.

— Proverbs 16:18

Arrogance leads to nothing but strife, but wisdom is gained by those who take advice.

— Proverbs 13:10 CSB

The LORD detests all the proud of heart. Be sure of this: they will not go unpunished.

— Proverbs 16:5

But he gives us more grace. That is why Scripture says: "God opposes the proud but shows favor to the humble."

— *James 4:6*

You save the humble but bring low those whose eyes are haughty.

— *Psalm 18:27*

You rescue an oppressed people, but your eyes are set against the proud—you humble them.

— *2 Samuel 22:28 CSB*

The LORD Almighty has a day in store for all the proud and lofty, for all that is exalted (and they will be humbled).

— *Isaiah 2:12*

God doesn't look favorably on a proud heart. When we put ourselves in god-like positions, which pride does, we invite trouble. God shows favor to the humble. Yet no one can flip a switch and become humble in a day. We'll never arrive by saying, "I'm going to try really hard to be humble today." Rule-following won't work. That's religion. But giving up and doing our own thing won't work, either. That's arrogance.

RELIGIOUS HYPOCRISY AND SELF-RIGHTEOUSNESS

Jesus is not a fan of religion. While on earth, his sharpest rebukes were given to religious people. In Matthew 23, he called them "blind guides," "hypocrites," "snakes," and people who "look beautiful on the outside but on the inside are full of the bones of the dead and everything unclean" (v. 27).

There's a famous story in the Bible about a father and his two sons.[18] The younger son demanded his inheritance early and left town to squander it with wild living. Once the money dried up, he headed home to his father because he was hungry. The older son, on the other hand, was dutiful, working hard for the father for many years. But upon the return of the younger brother, the older one became angry because a party was thrown and some of the best resources were used to welcome the young prodigal back. What's going on in this story?

The younger son is clearly in the wrong for leaving and blowing his inheritance. While reading the story, it's easy to look at this son and ask, "How could he have done such a foolish thing?" But the older, rule-following son is in a similar predicament. Even though he obeyed his father outwardly for years, his heart was not for the father but rather for what the father could give him. Henri Nouwen provides some helpful commentary on this story:

> The lostness of the elder son...is much harder to identify. After all, he did all the right things. He was obedient, dutiful, law-abiding, and hardworking... Outwardly, the elder son was faultless. But when confronted by his father's joy at the return of his younger brother, a dark power erupts in him

> and boils to the surface...
>
> There are many elder sons and elder daughters who are lost while still at home. And it is this lostness—characterized by judgment and condemnation, anger and resentment, bitterness and jealousy—that is so pernicious and damaging to the human heart... There is so much frozen anger among the people who are so concerned about avoiding "sin."...
>
> I recognize the elder son in me. Often I catch myself complaining about little rejections, little impolitenesses, little negligences. Time and again I discover within me that murmuring, whining, grumbling, lamenting, and griping that go on and on even against my will.[19]

Self-righteousness and religious hypocrisy are as deadly today as they've ever been. We are not immune. We think that by "following the rules," as it were, we deserve a party. We want the Father to make much of us and to rejoice because of our perceived obedience. But as this story helpfully illustrates, God doesn't give brownie points for outward appearances. He gives grace from the bounty of his heart. He is not pleased by showiness if our hearts are far from him. But his heart draws near, despite our best or worst efforts.

God wants people who are generous, merciful, kind, and humble. He wants people to experience his love. Jesus modeled these characteristics perfectly. When we huddle in various communities, whether socioeconomic, political, or religious in nature, we typically grow in arrogance, not humility. Self-righteousness not only blinds us to the needs of the world, but it also frustrates our ability to perceive God's love.

When we engage with others, we should ask whether we're genuinely focused on their needs or secretly hoping to benefit in some way from the interaction. Sometimes our concern for others is an attempt to earn favorable social status or gain control of a situation or relationship.

Consider generosity. When we give, are we doing so from a posture of obedience or to receive the applause of others? Jesus taught that giving should happen in such a way that our left hand is unaware of our right hand's actions (Matthew 6:3). In essence, we shouldn't shout our generosity from the rooftops. It shouldn't matter if people know we gave anything. Jesus says our giving should happen in secret. It's between us and the Lord.

Or consider prayer. We can become self-righteous in our public prayers, whether praying for a meal, leading a small group, or comforting a friend in need. Some people excel at praying—their words are eloquent and biblical. But it's possible to be good at praying while having a heart far from the Lord. Jesus says we shouldn't pray to be seen by others. Our prayers should be directed to God alone. Sure, they can and often do encourage others. But at the end of the day, without God at the center of our prayers, we're only offering words to people. Words can only take a person so far. But when God is the recipient of our prayers, the unimaginable is possible.

When we encourage someone with prayer, we say, in essence, "You matter. God loves you." When we give to others, we say, "You're valuable. God sees you." But we rarely value people the way God does.

WHAT MAKES PEOPLE VALUABLE?

We measure people's value in strange ways. If a lady has a BMW, we assume she's wealthy. If she drives a twenty-year-old beater, we assume she's poor. But God doesn't look at outward appearances (1 Samuel 16:7). He's more concerned about the condition of our hearts than the car in our driveway.

Although we're good at outward appearances, we're bad at addressing our interior woes. Much of what happens in our hearts goes unaddressed, in many cases haunting us until the grave. We hide our true selves from others, keeping our distance, lest they discover our wounds. Instead of doing the difficult heart work, we stay above the surface, polishing our trophy cases. We convince ourselves that if our inner world became known, we'd lose all value.

But what makes people valuable? Is it their ability to keep it all together? Is it the size of their bank account or their lifetime achievements? Are people valuable based on where they live, what they drive, and who they know? Should value be assessed pragmatically, placing higher levels on those who produce praiseworthy things?

God doesn't value the things the world values. According to Scripture, all people possess value because God loves them. Furthermore, all people deserve respect because God created them in his image. Regardless of their failures or accomplishments, people have intrinsic value.

Christians, perhaps most of all, should stop judging people based on their outward appearances. Is somebody wealthy? Great. Good looking? Fine. If such things vanished, would that person still be valuable? Absolutely!

Nancy Pearcy first opened my eyes to personhood theory in her book, *Love Thy Body*. According to this theory, "just being

A HEART OF HOLINESS

biologically part of the human race…is not morally relevant. Individuals must earn the status of personhood by meeting an additional set of criteria—the ability to make decisions, exercise self-awareness, plan for the future, and so on…. Only those who meet these added conditions qualify as persons."[20] In other words, a human being is only a person if they bring value to the world or can express a desire to be something or someone.

Personhood theory claims that human life, in and of itself, is morally insignificant. It doesn't matter if people have heartbeats or blood flowing through their veins, but only that they can express themselves in ways that give meaning to the world around them. According to Pearcy, this theory is responsible for much of the gender confusion, abortion debates, and euthanasia nightmares we see in our world today.

If we believe in personhood theory, that means as soon as we are unable to produce something valuable to society, we must be disposed of. If we're in the womb, we can be killed. If we're elderly and homebound, we may be humans, but we're no longer persons.

Understanding God's measure of value would produce an equality in our world that is severely lacking. If all people are valuable because they're made in God's image, then what they do, who they know, the money they earn, or their age make no difference to their worth. We'd all be infinitely valuable—neither Jew nor Gentile, slave nor free, male nor female, but all would be one, especially those in Christ Jesus (Galatians 3:28).

Imagine a world without division. Imagine a world without hate. Imagine a world where everyone knew, beyond the shadow of a doubt, that they were loved, valued, and worthy.

People are valuable because God loves them. It's really that simple. We don't have to produce anything to earn favor with God. He created us, and he is crazy about us. The dichotomy between human being and "person" is demonic and grossly unbiblical.

WHEN PRESSING "UNFOLLOW" IS NOT AN OPTION

Failing to recognize the origin of value creates division on many levels. It's the reason for much of our social unrest. We can't get along. We don't talk things through. Instead of cordially working through disagreements, we ignore people or seek to unfollow them, like life is a social media account.

Social media was created, in part, to connect people. I don't think it's working. Such platforms have created environments where people disconnect by canceling opposing viewpoints. For instance, if we see something we don't like online, we unfollow it. When people say offensive things on a given social platform, we block them. Viewpoints we find appalling are easily avoidable on social media, and such actions cause real issues in day-to-day, face-to-face life.

One of the oddest developments I've seen in recent years is how people feel personally attacked when an opinion of theirs is challenged. A sure way to get blasted with derogatory remarks is to disagree with someone on a given topic. What was once considered a simple disagreement now escalates to a shouting match with no resolution.

I once heard a guy in a grocery store loudly proclaim that a man who cheats on his spouse is "despicable and in need of mental help." While I certainly agree that cheating on your spouse is wrong, I also know sin lurks in every human heart. I decided to push back a bit by stating, "We're all capable of such actions."

The guy lost it. I was not expecting what happened next.

"That's ridiculous! It's offensive," he shouted, so that every

A HEART OF HOLINESS

customer could hear. "You're a scumbag. I would never do such a thing!"

I grabbed my items and left the store before anyone realized I was the wretched person being addressed. These are strange times, indeed.

What do we do when an opposing viewpoint is not encountered on a screen but rather face-to-face? What do we do when a coworker disagrees on a matter we deem important? How do we interact with an instructor who promotes an idea different from the one we've held since childhood? How might we encounter a disagreement without losing our cool in public places?

We can't simply unfollow people or block their ideas. The real world doesn't grant us that option. If we interact with people at all, we'll be confronted with something we disagree with. We must learn to work through our differences. We can't plug our ears and close our eyes. We shouldn't walk out of a situation to avoid confrontation. Thankfully, the Bible provides some direction.

In the church, we're told to be one in spirit and mind (Philippians 2:2). Unity is a big deal. Jesus certainly thought so, as evidenced in his prayer in the seventeenth chapter of John. It should be for us as well. Not only should we unite around Christ, but we should also be imitators of him. Jesus modeled humility perfectly, and he valued others consistently.

Though the world is divided, Christians are called to interact with it in different ways. Instead of avoiding difficult people, we should pursue them with love. Instead of frowning at their lifestyle choices, we should offer a kind word. Instead of holding grudges, we should grant forgiveness. Instead of shouting, we should turn the other cheek.

Love is about laying our lives down for the good of others (John 15:13). We're given opportunities every day to serve people in tangible, Christ-like ways. It's impossible to embody love

HUMILITY AND VALUING OTHERS

with resentment in our hearts. When we view others as threats or enemies, we lose the ability to love them.

In his letter to the church in Philippi, the Apostle Paul wrote some words that can help us pursue humility and love. He said we should do nothing out of selfish ambition or vain conceit. Our desire, in humility, should be to value others above ourselves. We should not look to our own interests but to the interests of others (Philippians 2:3-4). When we fixate on our own interests, discord ensues. On the contrary, if we look to the interests of others, harmony and unity follow.

Jesus said he came not to be served, but to serve and give his life as a ransom for many (Matthew 20:28; Mark 10:45). It's a counter-cultural way to live. Everyone will know we follow Jesus if we love one another (John 13:35). There is work for us to do. The Spirit of God will assist us to that end.

When we are faced with unpleasant people or ideas and opinions that clash with our own, we have two options available to us. We can reflect the heart of the world by fighting and dividing, or we can unite around the person and work of Jesus by loving, serving, and laying our lives down for the good of others.

Let's stop looking for the unfollow button. Let's avoid selfishness and vain conceit, and rather, in humility, value others above ourselves.

CHAPTER 4

ON NOT LOVING THE WORLD

Do not love the world or anything in the world. If anyone loves the world, love for the Father is not in them.

—1 John 2:15

Growing up, I loved the sport of skateboarding. I was enamored by the culture, clothing, and language. Everything about it spoke to my need for plowing my own course and avoiding anything that resembled conformity. I wanted to live counter-culturally, off the radar, to the beat of my own drum.

In those days, most of my time was spent learning tricks and researching the latest skate companies. I vividly recall the joy I felt when a UPS driver dropped a package at my doorstep containing a new skateboard—the components of which I spent hours selecting from a magazine designed to sell lots of stuff to young, gullible skaters.

After skating all day, I'd huddle with friends around the television to play Tony Hawk's Pro Skater or watch the X-Games, a competition featuring the best skateboarders in the world. I knew I would be the next Tony Hawk. I was destined to be a famous professional skateboarder. I just knew it. With grit and passion, I could conquer the world of skating.

Even though I spent years practicing and developing skills, my dreams of stardom never materialized. It didn't take long to feel crushed by the realization that I'd never be a famous skateboarder, regardless of how adamant I was about it. I failed, and it had nothing to do with my grit or passion. I worked hard, perfecting my arsenal of tricks, but it only led to burnout and frustration.

It's good to develop God-given talents. Good stewardship honors God. However, as we've already discussed in this book, issues arise when we attach our affections to things of this world apart from any connection to God or his glory. At its core, that's what I was doing with skateboarding. It became my identity, my everything. I didn't need God.

We all have a propensity to set our affections on things of this world. It happens all the time. We often find our hope, identity, and purpose in the things we do and love. Sometimes it looks like trusting in our own wit; other times, it's placing too much value in the stuff we own. When this occurs, we're loving the world and the things in it.

In her commentary on the epistles of John, Marianne Meye Thompson states that worldliness looks like a constant rejection of God's claims in favor of our own values and desires.[21] In essence, when we choose worldliness, we push God out of our lives and replace him with other things. This replacement of God is subtle yet powerful in its ability to wreak havoc in our lives. If we succeed by the world's standards, we may become conceited and live as if we're God, sovereign and in control, succumbing to a self-deception that is fatal to our soul. On the

ON NOT LOVING THE WORLD

other hand, if we fail by the world's standards, we may become miserable and adopt a "woe is me" attitude, spending our days like victims and demonizing those who appear successful.

We were created for God, not this world or its desires. As Saint Augustine famously said, our hearts are restless until they find rest in God. If we want to experience real joy and true freedom, we must seek him above everything else.

Unfortunately, most of us fall in and out of worldly patterns throughout our lives. The world and its desires are enticing. Our sin is always lurking. The pressure from the world feels impossible to combat, but we must combat it. In Romans 12:2, Paul says,

> *Do not conform to the pattern of this world, but be transformed by the renewing of your mind. Then you will be able to test and approve what God's will is— his good, pleasing and perfect will.*

Additionally, James 4:4 makes things crystal clear.

> *You adulterous people, don't you know that friendship with the world means enmity against God? Therefore, anyone who chooses to be a friend of the world becomes an enemy of God.*

Being God's enemy doesn't sound like a great life choice.

In what follows, I'd like to look at the Apostle John's command to not love the world. As with all Scripture, we can learn important lessons about life and holiness from his words. To drive his point home, John gives one command followed by three reasons, or, if you'd like, three arguments.

ONE COMMAND AND THREE REASONS

Here's the command, found in verse 15a: "Do not love the world or anything in the world." It's not a piece of advice. He's telling us what to do, how to go about our business, how to live our lives.

In the New Testament, the word "world" is the Greek word *kosmos*. It can mean different things in different places. For instance, world can mean the universe or material world. It can also mean the people of the world, such as in John 3:16, where God so loved the world. In 1 John 2:15, the word means "an evil system, organized under the dominion of Satan and not of God."[22] That's the world we're told not to love. It's corrupt and run by dark spiritual forces. As children of light, we should avoid engaging in darkness (1 Thessalonians 5:4-5). No matter the cost, we should walk in the light as God is in the light (1 John 1:7).

At this point, I hear several sincere readers saying, "Of course. I don't want anything to do with that world. I'm just trying to do my best, you know? I'm just trying to live a happy life." Yet it's possible to love this world without realizing what we're doing. Satan is a liar. The evil system under his control runs a monopoly on deception. His voice often sounds like ours. At times, it can even sound like the voice of Jesus. If Satan can get us off track, even in ways that appear innocent to us, he'll gladly do it. He couldn't care less about the means, only the results.

Therefore, as a reminder of who we are in Christ, the Apostle John goes on to give three reasons why we shouldn't love the world.

First, love for the world is incompatible with love for God. In verse 15b, we are told that if anyone loves the world, love for the Father is not in them (1 John 2:15). We cannot have it both ways. Many try to obtain a balance between love for the world and love for God. Yet this verse clearly teaches that love for God and love for the world can't happen simultaneously. If we become friends with the world, we become enemies of God (James 4:4). Also, Jesus said we can't serve two masters; we'll either hate one and love the other, or we'll be devoted to one and despise the other (Matthew 6:24). We've got to live radically and counter-culturally. When the world mocks us for pursuing holiness, we've got to keep our eyes on Jesus, our heavenly reward.

Christians are children of God, rescued and redeemed by Jesus himself. Our inheritance is eternal. We get all the riches, wonder, and joy of heaven. It's absurd, therefore, to stake our lives on things that pass away—things of this world.

When we continue reading, we see John's second argument against worldliness and his own definition of that word. He claims that worldliness is not an external problem but rather an internal one that produces in us selfishness, ungodliness, and arrogance. In other words, our outward behavior isn't what makes us worldly. Our worldliness comes from our interior world, the desires of our hearts.

In verse 16, John highlights the lust of the flesh, the lust of the eyes, and the pride of life as issues that arise from within a person. What John is doing is borrowing from one of Jesus' teachings found in Mark 7:21-22.

> *For it is from within, out of a person's heart, that evil thoughts come—sexual immorality, theft, murder, adultery, greed, malice, deceit, lewdness, envy, slander, arrogance and folly. All these things come from inside and defile a person.*

Selfishness, ungodliness, and arrogance come from the heart. They arise from within and cause us to misplace our love. Christians are marked by different characteristics. They possess what the Bible calls the fruit of the Spirit: love, joy, peace, patience, kindness, goodness, faithfulness, gentleness, and self-control (Galatians 5:22-23 CSB), a completely different paradigm than the world's.

Because of our culture's incessant grasping for possessions, it's worth mentioning that "the pride of life" mentioned in John's letter is all about feeling secure in the things we own and boasting about the luxuries at our disposal. Perhaps you know people like that, who place far too much significance in their homes, cars, financial stability, summer vacations, clothing, education, or careers. It is not wrong to own nice things. Not at all. It is wrong when nice things own us. There's a big difference.

I once met a guy who never stopped talking about his travel resume. He'd been all around the globe numerous times. It didn't take long to realize this man was in love with the world. I enjoyed many of his stories and was fascinated by other parts of the world. But this man's love for travel was more than a hobby or something that brought joy; it was his identity. He measured his worth by his ability to travel. This sort of all-consuming, stake-your-life-on kind of love is what John is speaking of when he says, "Do not *love* the world or *anything* in the world" (emphasis added).

John reserves his best and most compelling reason, found in verse 17, for last. He says the world and its desires pass away, but whoever does the will of God lives forever.

Life as we know it has an expiration date. We would be wise to heed this insight. Jesus warned us about misplaced treasure. Instead of exhausting ourselves for treasure that will ultimately fail us, we should seek treasure in heaven, where moths and rust do not destroy and where thieves do not break in and steal (Matthew 6:19-20). He said where our treasure is, there our heart will be also (Matthew 6:21). Apart from Christ, anything we place our affections in will pass away—our friends, our family, our careers, our stuff, our very lives.

The world and its desires can't fulfill us like Jesus can. The world promises much but delivers little. Jesus promises everything and delivers beyond our wildest dreams. Everything the world seeks will pass away. It will die. Everything Jesus offers will last forever.

> *For, "All people are like grass, and all their glory is like the flowers of the field; the grass withers and the flowers fall, but the word of the Lord endures forever."*
>
> *— 1 Peter 1:24-25*

If we are not to love the world and our biggest problem is internal, not external, how are we to obey John's command?

Timothy Keller wrote some fascinating words about our biggest problem and the solution to it.

> We love to be our own saviors. Our hearts love to manufacture glory for themselves. So we find messages of self-salvation extremely attractive, whether they are religious *(Keep these rules and you earn eternal blessing)* or secular *(Grab hold of these things and you'll experience blessing now)*. The gospel comes and turns them all upside down. It says: *you are in such a hopeless position that you need a rescue that has nothing to do with you at all.* And

A HEART OF HOLINESS

> then it says: *God in Jesus provides a rescue which gives you far more than any false salvation your heart may love to chase.*[23]

If we attach our affections to this world, we'll spend eternity separated from the love of God; however, if we attach our affections to the person and work of Jesus, we'll spend eternity in God's presence, where light and hope collide.

I pray we heed the words of John and choose our love wisely. Let's not mess around with the world's trivialities, even though they're so attractive. Let's respond to the gospel and give our lives to Jesus. We're not promised tomorrow, but if we give everything we are to him, we're promised a beautiful inheritance.

The gospel, literally, the good news, addresses all of life's dilemmas. Jesus died in our place for our sin so that we can experience abundant life. We can't flee our sinful hearts without first surrendering them to Jesus. He paid for my sin and your sin on the cross. When we give our lives to him, he gives us hope and a future beyond anything this world can deliver. If you've never done that, I pray you do so now. It's not too late. This is the single most important decision you'll ever make.

EIGHT WAYS TO NOT LOVE THE WORLD

If we receive what God in Christ has done for us on the cross, our future is sealed with his promised Holy Spirit (Ephesians 1:13). He will empower us to walk this stuff out. God can do immeasurably more through us than all we can ask or imagine (Ephesians 3:20).

In what follows, I want to get super practical, helping us live in such a way that our hearts radically desire God, not the world and its desires. Here are eight things we can do to not love the world:

1. Surrender every aspect of life to God.

This tip is broad, so we'll start with it first. If we don't surrender every aspect of our lives to God, we'll love the world, intentionally or not. We're made to worship. We'll either worship the Creator or some created thing (Romans 1:25). If we don't desire God, we'll desire something else. Therefore, it's only proper that whatever we do, whether it's eating, drinking, sleeping, or planning our future, we do it all for the glory of God (1 Corinthians 10:31). That's why we exist. We're made for God's glory (Isaiah 43:7).

Consider work. What might God want to accomplish through us in our workplace? How might God be leading us to bless the poor through our income? In what ways might God want to use our influence and abilities for the good of others? If we only consider our needs, we'll miss opportunities to bless the world with the love of Christ. God has a perfect plan for placing us where he did. He can use our employment in wonderful ways.

Consider our residence. Is our home a place where people can experience the love of God? Are we tangibly loving our neighbors, or do we find ourselves comparing our stuff to theirs? How might God want to use our homes to bless those with less? Our dining room tables can be a holy space where people can meet the living God. Our spare bedroom can be a wonderful way to shelter someone in need. Having a nice house is a blessing, but if we're not careful, that space can create in us an attitude of self-centeredness instead of an attitude of mercy toward others.

Consider possessions. How might God be leading us to downsize and declutter so that our treasures are in heaven, not in a storage unit? Perhaps we should give away our second vehicle to the stranger we see walking every day while we drive to work. Is it possible that God wants to free us from the worries of life, the deceitfulness of wealth, and the desires for other things by calling us to a more simplistic lifestyle?

2. Simplify your lifestyle.

Simplicity leads to freedom. It is "the only thing that sufficiently reorients our lives so that possessions can be genuinely enjoyed without destroying us."[24] When we fixate on our possessions, we become slaves to anxiety. For many of us, the fear of losing what we've worked hard to attain keeps us up at night. Because we've worked hard to earn it, we believe we must work hard to keep it. But this approach to life flies in the face of everything Jesus taught about wealth and possessions (Matthew 6:24). God is our provider, and he will take care of us if we seek his kingdom first and foremost (Matthew 6:25-33).

I once heard the story of a woman with a closet full of shoes. Although she owned many, she could never find a pair to wear. It wasn't that her closet was so cluttered that it was hard to find anything; rather, she couldn't decide because there were too many choices. That doesn't sound freeing to me. It sounds like bondage.

In what ways could you part with things for the sake of simplicity? What changes could you make that would lead to a place of freedom? How can you own things without them owning you?

ON NOT LOVING THE WORLD

3. Radically limit social media and streaming services.

I'm not on social media anymore. For me, social media was one of the main things that caused stumbling (Matthew 5:29). I found it hard to love people online when I'd see a comment promoting something I felt was harmful to human flourishing. I couldn't shake my desire to keep up with the Jones' when I saw others' vacation spots, home renovations, or parenting successes. I couldn't resist the urge to buy something I didn't need to impress people I didn't know. Social media exposed my love for the world in ways that led me away from holiness.

I'm aware of the reasons why people keep their accounts, such as mission work, staying connected to others, being light in darkness, or understanding the culture and being informed. Yet if I could measure my levels of joy without social media, the increase would be significant. Life is better without seeing everyone's edited, picture-perfect lives.

How might social media be causing you to love the world? How can you set healthy boundaries around the use of it? What about Netflix, YouTube, or other streaming services? How might they be forming you into the image of the world?

4. Don't engage in gossip or slander.

Part of the reason why social media is so addicting is because it's full of gossip and slander, and we're drawn to that kind of stuff. Sadly, I can think of times when I clicked on an ad because someone's weakness was exposed; or overheard a conversation and wanted in on the details; or spoke about a person behind their back in a way that was untruthful. Whether it's social media or the breakroom at work, gossip pulls us in.

Scripture makes it clear that such behavior is not befitting

A HEART OF HOLINESS

for a child of God.

> *Whoever slanders their neighbor in secret, I will put to silence; whoever has haughty eyes and a proud heart, I will not tolerate.*
>
> *— Psalm 101:5*

> *Do not let any unwholesome talk come out of your mouths, but only what is helpful for building others up according to their needs, that it may benefit those who listen.*
>
> *— Ephesians 4:29*

> *Nor should there be obscenity, foolish talk or coarse joking, which are out of place, but rather thanksgiving.*
>
> *— Ephesians 5:4*

> *Those who consider themselves religious and yet do not keep a tight rein on their tongues deceive themselves, and their religion is worthless.*
>
> *— James 1:26*

Gossip and slander are the love languages of a sinful world. It's becoming more common, not less. Because our call is to not love the world, we shouldn't fall into its bad habits. We can't allow our tongues to rob us of our pursuit of holiness.

Some great questions to ask ourselves during conversation

are: Are my words building others up according to their needs? How are my words benefiting those who listen? Am I keeping a tight rein on my tongue? If we don't take intentional steps to avoid gossip and slander, we'll be drawn into their realm.

5. *Cultivate gospel humility.*

Cultivating gospel humility is about understanding how our brokenness affects the way we engage with the brokenness of the world. We all have wounds—places where we've been deeply hurt or downright lied to. We shouldn't ignore the reality of our wounds. If we refuse to acknowledge our need for help, we'll attach to the world in ways that are harmful to ourselves and those around us.

First, we'll do harm to ourselves because we'll live a lie, believing we're better at navigating life than we actually are. Our decisions will be made from a place of deception and pride, not gospel humility. We'll think more highly of ourselves than we ought to and look down on others when they fail or fall short.

Second, we'll harm others because our interactions will be inauthentic. They'll not receive God's mercy through us but rather a counterfeit version of ourselves that resembles the world and its comparison and perfectionism. If we stop pretending, we'll be able to lead one another, with our brokenness and all, into the presence of Jesus—the place of forgiveness, wholeness, and rest. Jesus came into the world to rescue us. That's the greatest gift we possess. Jesus lives forever, interceding on our behalf. We must learn to decrease so that Christ may increase (John 3:30).

Gospel humility is an inspiring trait. When I'm around people who possess it, I can't help but worship Jesus. If we're not considering others as more important than ourselves, or if we're placing our interests above the interests of others, we'll love the world and demand a place in it. Love for the Father will not be in us. We'll spend our years trying to be someone other than who Christ says we are.

6. Seek neither poverty nor riches.

In Proverbs 30:8-9, we see Agur asking God to keep him from falsehood and lies, giving him neither poverty nor riches but only his daily bread. He asks this because he knows that riches could become too plentiful, causing him to disown God, or too scarce, causing him to steal, dishonoring the name of God. There is, undoubtedly, wisdom here for us.

In a world where the accumulation of stuff is seen as a sign of success, we must, as God's redeemed people, seek holy ground. We must guard our hearts against the cultural pressures of the day. This does not mean we should seek poverty. If God calls us to it, great, but to live in poverty as if such a lifestyle is God's standard for all Christians is simply not biblical. It will only do harm to us and the people around us. There are plenty of people in the Bible who had wealth, and lots of it. Think of Solomon or the women who supported Jesus' ministry. Poverty is not God's universal plan for his people.

On the other hand, to believe in the prosperity gospel is also unbiblical. This approach claims that God will financially bless those who do his will. Many use wealth as a litmus test for whether a person follows Jesus or not. Jesus wasn't wealthy, nor were many of his disciples. We can't turn wealth into a symbol of salvation. God is not pleased with us because we have wealth. Our riches could simply be a counterfeit god.

The best approach for Christians is to seek neither poverty nor riches.[25] This is holy ground. Like Paul, we should learn to be content with much, little, and everything in between (Philippians 4:11-13). Our greatest good is the presence, power, and person of Jesus in our lives for all our days. Nothing in life can compare to the riches that will be ours in heaven. Our very great reward is God himself (Genesis 15:1). To seek poverty or riches is to miss the King and the kingdom.

7. Observe the Sabbath.

For many of us, a nap should be in the immediate future. We need rest. We are not God, who doesn't need it, but he rested anyway to teach us a valuable lesson: He can run the universe without our constant motion.

The word Sabbath comes from the Hebrew word *Shabbat*, which simply means to stop. In ancient Israel, God's people were commanded to stop all the commotion in their lives—the work, the worry, the stress, the constant seeking after things of this world—once a week. How life-giving would this be for us today? How many of us would greatly benefit from stopping for a day? John Mark Comer has an excellent chapter about this in his book, *The Ruthless Elimination of Hurry.* He says,

> Sabbath isn't just a twenty-four-hour time slot in your weekly schedule; it's a *spirit* of restfulness that goes with you throughout your week. A way of living with "ease, gratitude, appreciation, peace and prayer." A way of working from rest, not for rest, with nothing to prove. A way of bearing fruit from abiding, not ambition.[26]

During Sabbath rest, we delight in God. We can use our time to take a nap, eat great food, laugh with our children, worship with our brothers and sisters in Christ, and do whatever makes our souls stand on their tiptoes. Sabbath is an amazing gift in our age of hurry. It can also prepare us to engage in our eighth (and last) step: fixating on eternity.

8. Fixate on eternity.

Perhaps the best way to not love the world is to stop thinking about it all together. Such an act requires the empowering work of God's Spirit, no doubt, but we can and must fixate on eternity.

> *Since, then, you have been raised with Christ, set your hearts on things above, where Christ is, seated at the right hand of God. Set your minds on things above, not on earthly things. For you died, and your life is now hidden with Christ in God. When Christ, who is your life, appears, then you also will appear with him in glory.*
>
> *— Colossians 3:1-4*

Heaven will be amazing. Words can't describe the joy we'll feel upon arrival. We must train ourselves to ponder the wonders of heaven again and again. The terrors of this life are fading. Our future home awaits. We'll soon rest in the arms of God, savoring the goodness of his creation. Forever.

CHAPTER 5

HEARING AND DOING

But be doers of the word and not hearers only, deceiving yourselves.

— *James 1:22 CSB*

One of the greatest joys of my life is being "daddy" to six amazing girls. At times, I'm the silly dad, running around the living room like a monster trying to catch little people; other times, I'm the storyteller, reciting the journey of a bear who runs into the forest for honey and shares the same name as the little person listening in. These moments are priceless. My guess is that they're the ones I'll look back on and wish I could experience again and again.

There are times, however, when I'm a killjoy—sending my daughters to bed early without the fun activity I promised beforehand. These moments typically include me shouting, "That's it! Go to bed!"

Life would be better if my children obeyed my instructions the first time. They're sweet kids and pretty good listeners. Sometimes, though, my words fall on deaf ears.

A HEART OF HOLINESS

"Girls, please pick up the living room before mom gets home." "Ok, dad," they agree in unison.

A few minutes later, I'm back in the room, projecting like a bull horn.

"Girls! Why are you doing front flips off the couch? And why is the living room still a mess?"

As children of God, our relationship with the Father is similar. He gives us instructions in his Word, yet we ignore the demands they place on our lives. We hear the words but don't obey them.

Thankfully, God is patient and kind. He doesn't scream at us or send us to bed early. The Bible says his kindness leads us to repentance (Romans 2:4). He allows us to respond to his love.

Because God loves us and is slow to anger, we should ask the following questions: How do we change at the heart level? How do we change from people who hear the Word to people who obey it?

Sadly, there are people who approach the Bible from an intellectual standpoint only. They don't let it disrupt their lives or penetrate the inward parts of their being. God, however, isn't impressed with mere head knowledge. He certainly wants us to use our brains, but not to the exclusion of our obedience. God doesn't look favorably on the person who only recites Bible verses, but rather on the person who is "humble, submissive in spirit, and trembles at my word" (Isaiah 66:2 CSB).

At its core, I'm convinced our obedience, or lack thereof, is a discipleship issue. We obey God to the degree we're committed to him. We obey God when our motives, by the power of the Holy Spirit, change from seeking our ways to seeking his. Unless we surrender to Jesus, following him regardless of the trajectory, we'll never put Scripture into practice.

FOLLOW ME

Life will always be all about Jesus. What he's done. What he's doing. What he'll continue to do. If we belong to him, every detail of our lives is called for.

Jesus says, "Follow me." Our job is not only to hear his words but to move into action. Disciples hear the Word *and* obey it.

Some theologians have defined discipleship as apprenticing under Christ. The goal is literally Christlikeness. We yearn to be *like* the master. We long to know his ways and live the life he would live if he were us.

In his excellent book, *Practicing the Way*, John Mark Comer clarifies that the word *disciple* is a noun, not a verb. More than being something that happens to us or something that we do, a disciple is who we are. We can't *disciple* a person any more than we can *Christian* him.[27] Apprenticing under Jesus is about whole-life transformation. It's about receiving a new identity and becoming a person of self-giving love.

Therefore, discipleship happens every moment of every day—while brushing our teeth; while driving to work; while eating dinner; while taking out the trash or changing diapers; while talking with the barista at our favorite coffee shop; or while worshiping with others on Sunday morning. Disciples use their days and hours wisely. They give every moment of every day to Jesus as a sacrifice and offering of praise.

THE THREE ESSENTIAL INGREDIENTS OF DISCIPLESHIP

I spent a few years working at Trader Joe's. While there, I learned the importance of reading food labels, particularly the list of ingredients on the sides of packaging. Not only did knowing a product's key ingredients help me make better eating decisions, it also allowed me to assist customers with their dietary needs.

Ingredients are printed in order by quantity used. In other words, if sugar is listed first, diabetics should run. The main ingredient could kill them. The product might contain 90% sugar! The highest amount of an ingredient is listed first, and the lowest last. Basically, the first two or three ingredients on a list make up the majority of what we're eating.

Understanding what's in our food is important for several reasons. One super practical reason is to make sure we get what we want. For instance, if we're looking for foods high in protein, one or more of the first ingredients must be rich in protein. Likewise, if we want to consume products high in fiber, one or more of the first ingredients must contain fiber. We're not going to get much protein if the first two ingredients are sugar and high-fructose corn syrup.

Like ingredient lists, discipleship consists of some essential components. If these "ingredients" were removed, discipleship, according to Jesus, would cease to exist. Jesus gave the three essential ingredients of discipleship when he said:

> *Whoever wants to be my disciple must deny themselves and take up their cross and follow me.*
>
> *— Mark 8:34*

Deny Yourself

We live in the age of self. Entrepreneurs picked up on this trend years ago and created industries that feed our desire to build our little kingdoms on earth. Whether through social media or consumerism, fashion accessories or various status symbols, we spend lots of resources creating an image or brand, one we hope gives us an edge, a hint of influence, or a small slice of the pie.

Jesus says that if we want to be his disciples, our agenda must go. Following Jesus means unfollowing ourselves. It's a radical message in a self-centered world; however, according to Christ, we find life when we stop grasping for it (Matthew 10:39, 16:25; Mark 8:35). Discipleship begins with denying self.

There is little perceived cost associated with following Christ these days, at least in the West. Self-promotion triumphs over self-denial. If Jesus helps us along the journey to a fulfilling life, we add him to our list of spiritual guides. When he challenges our beliefs about life and culture, we reinterpret what he said or ignore it altogether. Syncretism, that is, the blending of multiple worldviews, has won the day. Sadly, Christians are largely unaware of its effect on their lives and faith.

Jesus will not accompany a smorgasbord of spiritual guides. He claimed to be the one true path to God (John 14:6). He is the Lord of our lives, or nothing at all. All other allegiances must cease when Jesus enters the picture. When we declare Jesus Lord of our lives, we're signing up for at least three things.

First, we trust him alone for salvation. Nothing else and no one else can save us. What Jesus accomplished on the cross was more than a thoughtful deed. He satisfied the just wrath of God by dying in our place for our sins. Jesus paid it all so we could have it all. Instead of our endless attempts to get right with God, we simply embrace the blood Jesus shed for us on the cross. We receive forgiveness. We don't achieve it.

Second, we die to self-centered ways and repent of selfish pursuits. Prior to Christ, the inclination of our hearts was

A HEART OF HOLINESS

evil all the time (Genesis 6:5). Indeed, our hearts are deceitful and desperately sick (Jeremiah 17:9 ESV). But now, instead of self-promotion, we seek the glory of God and the good of others. Everything post-conversion is done for the establishment of his kingdom.

It's not always easy, but thankfully, he gives us new desires and new hearts (Ezekiel 36:26). He gives us life to the full (John 10:10). When sin wrecks us yet again, we turn to Christ for forgiveness. We let him wash our wounds. We lock our eyes on Christ, knowing those who look back are unfit for service in the kingdom of God (Luke 9:62).

Third, we seek God's will in all of life, abandoning our need to be in control. Our decisions, such as who to marry, where to live, how to vote, when to say yes or no, and every other decision, are determined through the prayerful combing of Scripture. Jesus and the gospel take center stage in our lives. We pray continually for God's will to be done in our lives as it is in heaven.

Years ago, I spoke with a bookseller at a secular bookstore. I asked him if they had a copy of Deitrich Bonhoeffer's *Cost of Discipleship*. He laughed and said he didn't think discipleship had a cost. I smiled politely and carried on with my shopping. I wish I had told the clerk that following Jesus costs us everything. Nothing is to be kept back. We bring nothing, but we get everything. It's terrifying and incredible.

C. S. Lewis understood this dynamic of discipleship, writing about it in the closing of his classic book, *Mere Christianity*.

> Give up yourself, and you will find your real self. Lose your life and you will save it. Submit to death, death of your ambitions and favourite wishes every day and death of your whole body

in the end: submit with every fibre of your being, and you will find eternal life. Keep back nothing. Nothing that you have not given away will be really yours. Nothing in you that has not died will ever be raised from the dead. Look for yourself, and you will find in the long run only hatred, loneliness, despair, rage, ruin, and decay. But look for Christ and you will find Him, and with Him everything else thrown in.[28]

Take Up Your Cross

During the Roman Empire, a cross was the most offensive and brutal tool available for executions. Criminals were forced to carry their cross before being nailed to it. Sometimes, they hung for days in full view of the public eye. Rome used such tactics to express their authority and power over individuals. Rome was in charge, and everyone knew it.

Crucifixion forced a person to submit to another. Jesus called his disciples to take up their cross, proclaiming his authority over them. God is sovereign and has claimed the right to rule every human life surrendered to him. And, thankfully, he's not a brutal dictator. He's gentle and humble in heart (Matthew 11:29). He doesn't lead with an iron fist but with a wounded hand.

Living under the authority of Jesus has both radical and practical elements. For instance, it's radical to deny ourselves and pursue holiness. It seems foolish. First Peter 4:4 says people will act surprised when we don't join them in their reckless, wild living. They will heap abuse on us for taking the high road. Yet from a biblical standpoint, we'll reap a harvest if we don't become weary of doing good (Galatians 6:9). Furthermore, the

A HEART OF HOLINESS

Apostle Paul reminds us that "godliness has value for all things, holding promise for both the present life and the life to come" (1 Timothy 4:8).

There are many ways to live under the authority of Jesus. Our specific calls look different, but we're all called to follow him.

Follow Jesus

Following Jesus means going wherever he leads. It requires turning away from every other voice and seeking his will in all matters. Disciples do this today in numerous ways, but spending time in Scripture and belonging to a local church are top priority.[29]

Spending time in Scripture is critical for the man or woman of God. The Bible is God's inspired Word. Although it's about God, it's *for* God's people. We meet with the living God when we open our Bibles. We engage with his heart and learn from his ways. In Scripture, we see the clearest picture of who Jesus is. There's no better way to interact with God than through Scripture.

Let me provide three tips for reading the Bible:

1. Choose the right Bible translation.

If you're unfamiliar with the Bible, choosing a translation can feel daunting. A simple perusal through a Bible app or the Bible section of a local bookstore can overwhelm even the most seasoned reader. Many options exist.

Don't panic. All the major English translations can serve you well. Here's some advice. First, pick a translation that's easy and enjoyable to read. If your version is difficult to understand, find a different one. You won't read consistently if the words or sentence structures are challenging. Even with the best intentions, you'll lose steam.

Second, use multiple translations while engaging in serious study. Unless you're familiar with Greek and Hebrew, the primary languages of Scripture, using multiple translations can only help. I prefer the NIV, CSB, and ESV. Many great translations exist, but I'm most familiar with these three. Bible apps typically offer multiple translations, so you can access them whenever you'd like.

Lastly, even though reading multiple translations is helpful for serious study, it's wise to have one "go-to" translation. Use many for study, but memorize, read, and teach primarily from one. Like a good friend, get to know a translation as well as possible. Being able to finish someone's sentence is proof of closeness. Picking up on a person's quirks and mannerisms happens as we spend time with them. The same is true when we're immersed in a translation.

2. Avail yourself of Bible study tools.

If you spend time in Scripture, you'll come across parts that will make you scratch your head and ask, "What in the world is going on here?" That's normal. Every honest reader of Scripture has moments like these. Avail yourself of Bible study tools. Like translations, we're blessed with lots of material to aid in our studies. Let me suggest two tools.

First, every Christian should own a good study Bible. Study Bibles not only contain the text of Scripture but also provide other material such as text commentary, articles, book introductions, maps, cross-references, and, generally, a concordance. Having these items in one place is helpful when trying to understand what you're reading.

A study Bible with contributions from scholars representing numerous denominations is useful; that way, you can learn from the wider church as opposed to one theological tribe. Theology is important. It's good to know where you stand on certain doctrines, but learning from the whole church is better than learning from one strand of it. It keeps us humble and helps us acknowledge the worldwide influence of Christ's bride. It seems like more and more study Bibles are written with a theological tribe in mind, so it may be hard to find one like I'm describing. But do your best.

Second, invest in commentaries. Commentaries are written by scholars who've spent their lives studying the Bible. Having access to them will help you understand things about the Bible that are not obvious from the text. For instance, when reading an epistle (letter) in the New Testament, understanding the cultural background will help you pick up on themes woven throughout the text. Since New Testament letters were written two thousand years ago, we can't assume we understand everything about the authors' world. Therefore, seek help from others in the broader church.[30]

3. *Seek both formation and information.*

Formation and information go together. If we're learning, we're growing. But people often treat the Bible as a textbook, robbing themselves of the riches hidden in plain sight. I've fallen into this pattern many times. It zaps the joy out of Bible reading.

Information is great and easily accessible today. The Bible, however, is the living Word of God, not an information bank. It should be read as an act of worship. It should be the primary place where we meet with Jesus. If we approach Scripture as a textbook only, we'll miss its transforming power. I know people who've studied the Bible for years but don't have a thriving relationship with Jesus. They know a lot of information, but their lives remain unchanged.

Memorizing parts of the Bible is another path toward formation.[31] When we memorize something, it sinks into our spiritual DNA in ways that cursory reading doesn't. How many of us over the age of thirty can recite our childhood phone number? Or how about lyrics from a song we haven't heard in years but sung nonstop when we were children? If you don't practice Scripture memorization, consider taking the verses at the start of each chapter in this book and setting them to memory. You'll be richly blessed.

Another way to be formed by the Bible is by praying through it as you read. Because God is holy and his Word is holy, praying Scripture back to God glorifies him and edifies us. The Psalms are a great place to develop a prayer language. Even beginning prayers with "God, you say in your word that…" and then filling in the blanks with a promise or truth from Scripture is a powerful and formative way to pray. There is no right or wrong way to do this, but we should do it.

More could be said, but I want to turn our attention to belonging to a local church because it is another important way to follow Jesus today.

Jesus said, "I will build my church, and the gates of Hades will not overcome it" (Matthew 16:18). He is doing that now, building his church through the lives of people like you and me.

As we interact with God's redeemed people, whether through a Bible study, a small group, a service project, a mission trip, or some other ministry in our local church, we learn

A HEART OF HOLINESS

some valuable lessons about Jesus and ourselves.

First, Jesus was humble. He laid his life down for the good of others. As you'll recall, Jesus calls us to lay our lives down for each other as well, doing nothing out of selfish ambition or vain conceit (Philippians 2:3).

Second, the Spirit of God gives each of us gifts. We must use our gifts for the common good. Look at the following words from the Apostle Paul:

> *There are different kinds of gifts, but the same Spirit distributes them. There are different kinds of service, but the same Lord. There are different kinds of working, but in all of them and in everyone it is the same God at work. Now to each one the manifestation of the Spirit is given for the common good. To one there is given through the Spirit a message of wisdom, to another a message of knowledge by means of the same Spirit, to another faith by the same Spirit, to another gifts of healing by that one Spirit, to another miraculous powers, to another prophecy, to another distinguishing between spirits, to another speaking in different kinds of tongues, and to still another the interpretation of tongues. All these are the work of one and the same Spirit, and he distributes them to each one, just as he determines.*
>
> *— 1 Corinthians 12:4-11*

Our gifts thrive in the local church. They were given for the common good. When we utilize our giftings, with their intended end in mind, we model Christ to one another and to the world. It's part of what it means to be a disciple of Jesus. We give, love, and serve, and the world is changed by our actions. We'll explore the benefits of belonging to a local church more in the next chapter.

Don't miss the power of Jesus' words about discipleship. If we want to apprentice under him, we must deny ourselves, take up our cross, and follow him. There's no other way.

THE GIFT OF FRIENDS WHO KNOW THEIR BIBLE

A few years ago, I reconnected with a friend from childhood. We had lunch together and reminisced about the old days. When I came home that evening, my wife noticed I was using lingo she had never heard from me before. I was unaware of what I was doing. Unknowingly, I slipped into old habits from the years of being around this friend. That's how relationships work. We take on the mannerisms of those we spend time with. We can also take on aspects of their spiritual lives. It's important, therefore, to choose our friends wisely, especially if we're serious about growing in holiness.

We need people in our lives who know and obey the Bible, people who will encourage us to do the same. It's such a gift to have friends who know their Bible—men and women who can gently correct us when we err, remind us of great truths when we live lies, encourage us to greater depths when we plateau, and model life under the authority of God's Word.

In his book, *Deep Discipleship,* J. T. English argues,

> Community is indispensable to discipleship, but community is not discipleship. We cannot be disciples of Christ outside the context of community. However, we can be in community that is not

> teaching us to be disciples of Christ.[32]

In other words, simply hanging out with people, even Christians, does not translate into discipleship. We must surround ourselves with people who lovingly challenge us to be like Jesus. The best way to do that is to join a community of Bible hearers and doers.

None of us has Scripture mastered. We all need help navigating its terrain, plumbing its depths, and applying its commands. More than having a cheerleader at our side, a friend who knows her Bible is like a drink of cold water on a humid summer day—providing vitality to the heart, strength to the spirit, and sustenance for the journey. There are few relationships like those.

The Bible is God's inspired Word. Its perfect revelation was given to God's people for their instruction and edification. It explains what life is all about. It proclaims the truth of God's salvation through Christ. If we surround ourselves with people who love it, obey it, and share it with us, we'll be immensely blessed.

I regularly meet with a group of guys. These men know their Bibles. They also love Jesus. I've received many gifts from them, ranging from spiritual guidance to tangible help. The biblical guidance these men share through our time in prayer is the greatest blessing of all.

One guy has a grasp on the Old Testament that's inspiring. He shares stories from its pages as effortlessly as a leaf flowing down a stream. When we talk and pray together, he reminds us of the providence of God seen throughout Israel's history. I always leave our meetings yearning to know the Bible better.

My family has also experienced tangible blessings from these men. They are not just hearers of the word, but doers.

The Bible tells us faith is dead if it's not accompanied by works (James 2:17, 26). If we claim to have faith but don't meet the needs of others, especially when it's within our ability to do so, it's possible we don't possess the saving faith we claim to have. We may be deceived. These men have met some amazing needs in my family.

Another gift I've received from my Bible-believing friends is encouragement to dive deeper into the reality of God's kingdom. God is working in our world. We can join him in his redemptive work. My worldview is greatly shaped by my friends' surrendered lives. Their hunger for God is contagious. They refuse to settle for a shallow Christianity. They want to know Christ and him crucified (1 Corinthians 2:2). When I watch them lead at home, at work, and at church, I'm inspired to take Christ-like responsibility for my own life. Their lives display the power of God.

Friends who know their Bible are a gift. Few things in life compare. Do you have friends like these? If not, ask God. He doesn't want you to walk the Christian life alone. If you want to be his disciple, hearing and doing the Word, you'll need to get around Christians who can challenge you to do what it says.

Jesus said,

If you continue in my word, you really are my disciples. You will know the truth, and the truth will set you free.

— John 8:31-32 CSB

CHAPTER 6

WE NEED GOSPEL REMINDERS

Therefore, there is now no condemnation for those who are in Christ Jesus.

—Romans 8:1

It was a typical morning in our home. My daughters were taking the day by storm. I was running late.

"Look at George, daddy! He's right there," my six-year-old said as I reached for my work bag and headed out the door, barely deciphering her last sentence.

George is the name of a cardinal. The girls named all the animals in the neighborhood. There's George the cardinal, Spot the blue jay, Mrs. Whitetail the deer, Camo the rabbit, Dottie the squirrel, and Big Puffy the cat. I've seen them all except George. My daughter was determined to show him to me, and he was just perched on the bird feeder in front of our house. Except, I was too busy to notice.

I was late to a nine o'clock prayer meeting. You know, holy stuff.

As I approached the car, I realized I had left my hoodie be-

A HEART OF HOLINESS

hind and reluctantly headed back inside to retrieve it. I walked into a conversation that led to an important parenting lesson.

"Mommy, he didn't even listen," my daughter said with tears in her eyes. "Why don't you tell him how you feel?" my wife urged while eying me with disapproval. My daughter shook her head and stopped talking. She was holding back tears.

I blew it. I knew it instantly. Once again, I let my self-centeredness hurt someone I love dearly.

I could've beat myself up, believing I was the worst dad on the planet. I could've let lies wash over my mind, convincing me I'd never change. I could've told my daughter to respect my time, pretending I was the most important person in the room. But honestly, there's no sense in hiding flaws from my family. They know me better than anyone. I can't hide.

I apologized, and thankfully, she offered forgiveness. I hugged my little girl and assured her that next time would be different. Like parents do.

I made it to the prayer meeting. I wasn't late. I said some prayers that sounded holy.

Later that day, while reflecting on the morning, I sensed God saying, "Daniel, next time, get excited about the cardinal so that you can get excited about the girl who's excited about the cardinal." The words were corrective but also sweet in nature, not harsh. I sensed no trace of condemnation.

Condemning words can strike often. Accusations can arise without notice. Neither are from God.

"You're not good enough. You blew it. You'll never amount to anything. How could you do that? You're an idiot!" These are the types of words I expected to hear. At various times in life, such words have fallen from the sky, assaulting my mind for no apparent reason.

When I entered full-time ministry, I'd hear lies at the conclusion of my workdays. I'd believe I misrepresented God's Word or placed a burden on someone he never intended them to carry. I couldn't shake the feeling that I'd messed up. I believed lies about myself and even questioned my call to ministry. They were scary moments. One minute I was fine; the next, I was anxious and short-tempered with my family and friends. The experience was unhealthy for my mental state, but more importantly, it was unfair to those around me.

The accusations haven't gone away entirely. Thankfully, I've learned to battle such moments by preaching the gospel to myself over and over. I've learned to identify what's true and false about myself and the world around me. I'm keeping the gospel on repeat.

You may be wondering: What is the gospel? Can it help me in bad moments, too? What about accusations? Where do they come from? These are vitally important questions. Let's begin by exploring the gospel message.

HUMANITY'S GREATEST PROBLEM AND THE HOPE OF CHRIST

In recent years, our world has experienced numerous problems.[33] It seems like everywhere I turn, another crisis is being tackled, and more division is being created. Things such as global pandemics, racism, political angst, and debates surrounding gender and human sexuality will undoubtedly make it into the history books as the major cultural tensions of this decade.

Yet as bad as these problems have become, they're simply symptoms of a greater problem. In fact, every problem in history, whether social injustice, greed, slavery, etc., has its origin in this one underlying problem.

The Bible does not mince words. The greatest problem facing humanity is not racism, human trafficking, gay rights, greed, or even global pandemics. The greatest problem facing humanity is sin and death (Romans 5:12).[34]

When God created the world, death, disease, and decay did not exist. People lived in harmony with one another and God. Racism had no place, and deadly viruses were unfathomable. These problems, along with all the others, entered the cosmos when humanity, by its own choice, disobeyed the command of their Creator (Genesis 2:17). The book of Genesis records this disruption well (Genesis 3).

God never intended his creation to distance themselves socially or disrespect one another in any way. All our current issues are a result of humanity's rebellion against God.

Sin cannot be resolved by positive thinking, legislating morality, redefining personhood, or simply pretending it doesn't exist. Death cannot be conquered by dietary choices, exercise programs, or medical advances. We have a problem, and we need help from outside ourselves, our world systems, and our cultural perspectives.

The Bible says to deny sin is to live without truth and under deception (1 John 1:8). Sadly, we work hard to ignore our greatest problem because it's difficult to admit that we created it. We are the problem.

> *We all, like sheep, have gone astray, each of us has turned to our own way; and the LORD has laid on him the iniquity of us all.*
>
> — *Isaiah 53:6*

In the book of Jeremiah, the prophet claims the human heart is "deceitful above all things, and desperately sick (Jeremiah 17:9 ESV). Paul, in his letter to the church at Rome, said,

"For all have sinned and fall short of the glory of God" (Romans 3:23). David said he was conceived in sin and sinful at birth (Psalm 51:5). The same is true of you and me. Indeed, the Bible is full of verses that talk about the sin of humanity—that no one does good, not even one (Romans 3:12).

If we can't fix sin or avoid death, where should we turn for help? Is there hope?

Many people believe the remedy to our problem will be found when we reform government or legislate morality; however, as history has shown, our problems run deeper than any law, ideology, or political system. If the human heart is desperately sick and deceitful above all things, any human effort to resolve humanity's problems is doomed to fail. We can't fix what is broken. We need to be rescued from ourselves. Thankfully, the Creator of the universe hasn't left us to figure things out on our own.

Our only remedy is the person and work of Jesus Christ, God's only Son who came into the world to rescue us and offer eternal life (John 3:16). Jesus is our rescuer and our hope. The sooner we embrace Jesus as the all-sufficient rescuer, the sooner we'll begin seeing true and lasting reconciliation in our relationships with God and others.

Jesus died so that we could be reconciled to God. He died and was raised to reverse the curse of the fall in Genesis 3.

> *The righteousness of God is through faith in Jesus Christ to all who believe, since there is no distinction. For all have sinned and fall short of the glory of God; they are justified freely by his grace through the redemption that is in Christ Jesus.*
>
> *— Romans 3:22-24 CSB*

That's it. The greatest message in the history of the world. Not only is it the most important message, but it's also the only essential message.[35]

Jesus lived the life we couldn't live and died the death we should've died because he loves us and wants a relationship with us. By his wounds, we are healed (Isaiah 53:5). His death means the forgiveness of our sins, and his resurrection means the assurance of our hope. The gospel—the shed blood of Jesus on our behalf—is the remedy for humanity's greatest problem. We must preach it to ourselves regularly. Jerry Bridges offers some good advice.

> When you set yourself to seriously pursue holiness, you will begin to realize what an awful sinner you are. And if you are not firmly rooted in the gospel and have not learned to preach it to yourself every day, you will soon become discouraged and will slack off in your pursuit of holiness.[36]

GOOD NEWS IN LIGHT OF BAD NEWS

The gospel is good news in light of bad news. If we avoid the bad news (we are sinners and have made a mess of things), we'll never truly understand the good news (the cross of Jesus brings hope through reconciliation). The message of the gospel is "we are more wicked than we ever dared believe, but more loved and accepted in Christ than we ever dared hope."[37] That's it—wicked and loved, both at the same time. We're going to make mistakes and fall short, but Christ's love for us is greater than we can fathom, despite our wickedness.

We're not our best or worst moments. Whether we knock it out of the park or fail miserably, Christ's gracious heart moves toward us. When we blow it, the blood of Christ covers us with forgiveness and grace; when we "nail it," the nails that pierced the Son of God say more about our worth than all the congratulatory remarks thrown our way.[38]

Speaking the gospel to ourselves while sensing condemnation can act as a healing ointment for our guilty consciences. We're our worst critics, and our consciences regularly pronounce us guilty. It's frustrating. When we recall what Jesus did for us on the cross, when we allow the truth of his atoning sacrifice to invade our thoughts and hearts, and when we welcome the life-giving reality that God is for us, not against us, condemnation will slowly lose its influence, which in turn will make room for joy, peace, thankfulness, and life to the full.

Because of the cross of Jesus, God is not mad at us. He's not condemning us. We must recognize that reality, or we'll believe lies and feel condemned. Again, Jerry Bridges said,

> There are two "courts" we must deal with: the court of God in heaven and the court of conscience in our souls. When we trust in Christ for salvation, God's court is forever satisfied. Never again will a charge of guilt be brought against us in heaven. Our consciences, however, are continually pronouncing us guilty. That is the function of conscience. Therefore, we must by faith bring the verdict of conscience into line with the verdict of heaven.[39]

Bringing the verdict of conscience into line with the verdict of heaven is what the gospel does. It's not always easy. But, like anything in life, the more familiar we get with it, the more readily we'll turn to it. If the gospel is the only essential message, we need it more than anything else—more than money, more than fame, more than the fleeting pleasures of our flesh.

The other side of this equation is learning to speak the gospel to ourselves in moments of triumph. It's great to experience victories in life, perhaps especially in our work. Ministry work is no different. When things are going well with discipleship at our church, we'd be remiss not to celebrate it. When people engage with a community in the context of a small group, rejoicing should occur. When marriages are strengthened, when God's people are generous to the poor, when sin is repented of, and when people seek holiness, we should throw a party. Even angels in heaven experience joy when great victories are won (Luke 15:10). Yes, we should celebrate, but we should continue to preach the gospel to ourselves as well, particularly in these moments, or we may be overcome with pride.

Pride is one of the greatest sins we see in the Bible. Pride caused Satan to fall. Pride caused Adam and Eve to believe Satan in the garden, leading to humanity's curse. Pride caused the Israelites to receive a stark warning from God (Leviticus 26:19). Pride always leads to destruction (Proverbs 16:18). Anytime we think more highly of ourselves than we ought, pride lurks in our hearts.

Therefore, we must guard against pride in the midst of life's victories. The best way to avoid it is by speaking the gospel to ourselves during triumph. We shouldn't pretend we're the ones accomplishing great things, but rather, Christ, by his empowering gifts, is accomplishing great things through us.

Jesus did something extraordinary on the cross. We don't have to live in dark pits any longer. We can stop pretending to be righteous and own the fact that, in Christ, we already are.

That's the heart of the gospel message. But what about accusations? Let's turn there now.

THE ORIGIN OF ACCUSATIONS

God never forsakes his people. But unfortunately, we have an enemy who never forsakes lying. By familiarizing ourselves with his tactics, we can win the battle against accusations. We can achieve victory over Satan's destructive schemes.

In his letter to the church at Ephesus, the Apostle Paul counseled readers to wear the full armor of God. He clarified the origin of their struggle, claiming it was "not against flesh and blood, but against the rulers, against the authorities, against the powers of this dark world and against the spiritual forces of evil in the heavenly realms" (Ephesians 6:12). Because the Ephesians lived in close proximity—many living under the same roof—Paul wanted them to realize attacks are spiritual in nature, not physical. This insight should prove helpful for us today as well.

For instance, people don't need to feel undone by a sly remark from their in-laws or crushed by the verbal blows of an employer, as if they themselves were to blame for the angst. Evil spiritual forces are often at the heart of accusatory language. It may sound frightening; we may not like the conclusion; but the truth is, Satan is at work in our world. He wants nothing less than the destruction of everything pure, right, and godly. He's not for us. He's not our friend.

By moving their attention to the spiritual reality of life, Paul equipped his readers for a lifelong war. Likewise, our struggle with Satan will continue until we meet Jesus face-to-face. On that day, our enemy will be completely overtaken, losing his power and ability to cause any harm to God's people, real or perceived.

Satan is not dumb. He knows our struggle with sin. He'll use it against us as much as possible. But Satan is not the only reason for the accusations we hear; another is sin itself.

IN OUR WORST MOMENTS

As a pastor, I meet with people to remind them of the gospel. It's the best part of my job. But it's often heartbreaking, like when I sit with couples dealing with infidelity or some other sin threatening their relationship. Walking with people through forgiveness isn't easy, but it's essential gospel work.

I'm not a counselor. I generally preface these meetings with that fact. Counseling can help people in wonderful ways. I'm all for counseling, but I'm not a counselor. I'm a pastor. I represent Christ by caring for his flock. There's no better way to do that than by reminding God's people of the gospel's power. The gospel affects everything, not just our relationship with God. I've tried bringing the gospel into every aspect of my ministry.

I remember the first time I had one of these meetings as a pastor.[40] I sat with a married couple facing infidelity. A month prior to our visit, the man had a hotel room booked and was on his way to hook up with an ex-girlfriend. Even though he claimed to be a Christian, temptation arose in a moment of great weakness. It happens to everyone. Even Jesus faced temptation in every way, just like us, but he didn't sin (Hebrews 4:15).

The man said, "Something powerful came over me while driving to the hotel. It caused me to sweat and sense the weight of the thing I was doing. I knew I was making a big mistake." He lied for weeks regarding his whereabouts. He desperately tried to cover the whole thing up. After his wife did some investigating, including a phone call to the hotel, the man's actions became known. He was caught in a lie. He couldn't hide.

Through tears, he said, "How could this happen? I don't

understand how I got here." The weight of sin crushed him. He stopped making excuses. He knew he blew it and needed help. He repeatedly apologized to his wife and added, "I need to get right with God." He needed the gospel.

Sin is a powerful force. It can steer the ship of our lives. The Apostle Paul said we are enslaved to sin apart from the work of Christ in our lives (Romans 6:6). Without God's Spirit in us, we will sin. It's unavoidable.

According to Jesus, sexual immorality is grounds for divorce (Matthew 19:3-9). I don't want to sugarcoat the severity of this sin. I rarely advocate for divorce, but sometimes it's necessary. In this case, both parties wanted to reconcile and move forward with forgiveness.

The couple finished speaking, and then I explained the gospel from Romans 8:1. The man needed to know God wasn't mad at him. Condemnation isn't from God. Anyone in Christ has been forgiven of their sins, past, present, and future. There is no condemnation. None. I encouraged him to memorize this verse. I told him that, in moments of accusation, he'd need it like a soldier needs a weapon in battle.

But I wasn't only concerned about the man. His wife had been wronged. I wanted her to know that she too was known and loved by God. Yet forgiveness would cost her greatly. It cost God the life of his Son. It would cost her the emotional rollercoaster of anger, grief, feelings of abandonment, and heartache of all kinds—perfectly normal emotions during such scenarios.

Forgiveness isn't about forgetting the wrong done to us. It's irritating when people say, "We need to forgive and forget." That statement isn't biblical. Biblically speaking, we're tasked with forgiving and moving forward in Christ, even if we never forget the wrong done to us. For this couple, moving forward looked like many things (repentance, time, counseling, relationship building, etc.), but one very important aspect was living in community. They needed to get around other Christians.

THE VALUE OF CHRIST-CENTERED COMMUNITY

The man didn't attend church regularly, though his wife did. When I asked him about his absence, he said, "I just don't believe I have to go to a building to worship God."

His wife promptly chimed in, "Are you worshiping God outside of this building?" To which he admitted, "No, I suppose I'm not."

This interaction was interesting to me and led to a brief discussion about belonging to a church community where they'd be loved and reminded of the gospel. Although I agree that worshiping God has little to do with a building, I also know the safest place for Christians to exist is in the midst of a church community, which, for our church, includes worship in a building.

Scripture refers to God's people as sheep. If a person claims to be a follower of Christ, they are sheep of his flock. The thing about sheep is that they stink and stand really close to each other. They may not all look alike, but they all have similar inclinations. For instance, all sheep lack the ability to lead themselves anywhere safe. That's why they need a shepherd, so they don't go astray and get attacked by wolves.

According to the Iowa Sheep Industry Association, "sheep are prey animals. It is flocking together in large groups that protect sheep from predators because predators will go after the outliers in the flock."[41] Belonging to a church community keeps us from being outliers. Bob Tuttle, professor emeritus at Asbury Theological Seminary, has said, "If you get singled out, you get picked off." Surely that's reason enough to belong to a church community.

Jesus is a shepherd, not a life coach. He's not interested in making us better people if we're not interested in belonging to his flock. It's not about us. It's not our story. If Christians truly want to thrive, they must belong to a church community that preaches the gospel regularly. The safest place for Christians is right in the middle of a smelly flock, one led by the good shepherd himself, Jesus.

> *I am the good shepherd; I know my sheep and my sheep know me—just as the Father knows me and I know the Father—and I lay down my life for the sheep. I have other sheep that are not of this sheep pen. I must bring them also. They too will listen to my voice, and there shall be one flock and one shepherd.*
>
> *—John 10:14-16*

We need gospel reminders. Without the gospel, we'll be tempted and led astray. We'll hear, believe, and live lies. We all fall short, but the gospel is hope for weary sinners.

CHAPTER 7

WE CAN'T STAY YOUNG FOREVER

*Remember your Creator in the days
of your youth, before the days of trouble come
and the years approach when you will say,
"I find no pleasure in them."*

— *Ecclesiastes 12:1*

Our world is obsessed with youth and beauty. Lots of money is spent each year on beauty products to keep us looking young and agile. According to one report, the beauty industry is valued at an estimated $532 billion, and experts claim those numbers will continue to rise.[42]

Our obsession isn't surprising when you consider the cultural narrative in which we live. The narrative claims the good life is reserved for the young and beautiful. We see it on our movie screens. We view it on our social media feeds. We hear about it as we work, shop, and engage with friends and neighbors. It feels impossible to escape and is one of the reasons we're compelled to stare at a mirror. Yet the reality is that if we live long enough, our youth, and any beauty we possess, will flee, despite our best efforts to retain it.

WHEN YOUTH AND BEAUTY FLEE

Aging happens. If we live long enough, we'll get old. All of us. Many will look back on life and ask, "How did I get here?" Some will wonder, "When did the pages of life turn over? Why couldn't I detect it?" Whether we're seventy looking back on our fifties or forty looking back on our twenties, the reality of aging is bewildering, to say the least.

There's a line in John Mayer's song, "Stop this Train," where he sings,

> So scared of getting older. I'm only good at being young. So I play the numbers game to find a way to say that life has just begun.

I love that line. Like so many others from Mayer, the human condition is spoken of with vulnerability and honesty.

I relate to the tension. I've only been young. I have no idea what it's like to be old. My guess is that getting older is like staring into a mirror maze. There's wonder and disorientation. People think they see the route ahead, but, upon proceeding, they're stopped, rerouted, and receive blows to the head by the undetected walls in front of them.

Like a train in motion, we're headed toward a new land—a different environment with unknown possibilities and heartache. Short of the train stopping, we can't get off. We can't stay young forever, though many of us try, even late into our lives. Youth simply spreads its wings and flies away.

Can we properly prepare for the aging process? Is there a way to age gracefully and biblically? The answer is *yes* to both questions. The Bible provides wisdom for readers of all ages. No one is excluded.

In Ecclesiastes 12:1, the author instructs us to remember our Creator while we're young, before troubling times come and there's no pleasure to be found. We don't often consider it, but our bodies will break down as the years pass. It'll be harder to do things that come naturally now, like sitting, laying down, walking across a parking lot, getting in and out of the shower or bathtub, and a handful of other activities. It's sad how we take things for granted. We don't know what we have until it's gone.

The passage continues by using metaphorical language to describe all the ways our bodies decay and the latter years wane. Thankfully, verse one teaches us the key to living well now and in the future. It suggests we remember the one who created us so we can learn two truths: we're created on purpose, and our Creator is faithful.

We're Created on Purpose

First, we need to acknowledge that we're created beings. Our lives matter. We're not some cosmic accident. Because we're created by a Creator, our lives have purpose.

Consider a painter or an architect. When they design a work of art, whether a painting or a breathtaking skyscraper, they have a specific purpose in mind. Their creation may be for the enjoyment of others, to turn a profit, or to build a reputation, but either way, there was a purpose in the mind of the creator for the thing they created. It's also true of God, our Creator.

According to Scripture, we're created for his glory (Isaiah

43:6-7). We need to remember him and consider his purposes so we can live purposeful lives. If we live for anything other than God's glory, we may have fun in life, we may have influence, and we may reach the heights of success, but at the end of it all, we'll waste our lives. We'll fail to live the life for which we were created.

If we miss the truth that we're created on purpose, we'll also miss the joy our hearts desire. There is joy to be experienced when we glorify God with our lives—indescribable, all-consuming joy. There's nothing like living a joyful life. When we know why we're created and live life like we believe it, God is glorified, and we are wonderfully happy.

Our Creator is Faithful

Second, we should remember the faithfulness of our Creator. How has God provided for our needs? Can we think of specific ways he's come through for us? Can we remember the prayers he answered that changed the direction of our lives?

If we reflect on God's faithfulness regularly, it'll be difficult for troubling times to shake us. We'll be better prepared to ride out the storms of life because we'll be connected to the one who calms the storms. We're not alone. We have an advocate—a friend who promises to stay with us (Matthew 28:20).

Notice what the verse doesn't say. It doesn't say, "*if* the days of trouble come," but rather, "*before* the days of trouble come." It assumes troubling days are ahead. In other words, difficult times will arise in life. We can count on it. In fact, Jesus said,

> *In this world you will have trouble. But take heart! I have overcome the world.*
>
> *— John 16:33*

At the very least, this verse should keep us from panicking when something strange and unusual happens (1 Peter 4:12-19). Trouble will come upon Christians and take on many shapes and sizes. But we don't have to allow aging to alarm us. God has something sweet for us in the later years.

AGING WITH HOLY EXPECTANCY AND JOY

I've spent several years observing the elderly in hopes of gleaning some wisdom about the aging process in general and "being old" in particular. A definition of "elderly" should be more intricate and beautiful than age alone. We should avoid saying the thing so many of us say, namely, that an elderly person is an old person. I disagree.

I've noticed two types of elderly people: those who are on mission and those who aren't. My hypothesis is that those who lived their youth with daily surrender to Jesus live their later years with holy expectancy and joy, while those who lived their youth with anything other than Jesus burn out when their life goals, for better or worse, end.

When our eyes are fixed on that beautiful country God promises to all who trust in him, age can't deter us from radical joy.

As I write these words, I'm saddened by the death of Timothy Keller, one of the greatest authors, pastors, and theologians to come out of the American church in recent memory. After perusing various articles online giving him praise for a life well lived, I'm most encouraged by his final words. According to his son, Michael, Tim said, "There is no downside for me leaving, not in the slightest," and "I'm ready to see Jesus. I can't wait to see Jesus. Send me home." What sweet words from a man who understood the glorious riches awaiting him. He understood joy in Christ and eagerly awaited its fulfillment. He stayed on mission until the end.

I'm grateful for the older mentors I have, both those I know personally and those, like Timothy Keller, I've learned from but never met. They've taught me the importance of surrendering all to Jesus. When I observe their lives, I notice several important themes.

First, they recognize the brevity of life and use their time for Christ-exalting, redemptive work. How many of us spend our years exalting ourselves and putting our own agendas before Christ's? I, for one, have spent more time than I'd like to admit building my kingdom—one that, apart from Christ, will crumble. I often want to be made much of, be praised by others in the ministry world, or appear smarter than I really am. It's an exhausting and miserable way to live. Oh, how I wish I was more like my mentors, who understand that life is not about them.

C. T. Studd penned the famous words,

> Only one life, 'twill soon be past, only what's done for Christ will last.

I love those words. My wiser friends have taken them to heart and live them out regularly. Long gone are the days of making a name for themselves. Their one desire is to make much of Jesus and, when they meet him face-to-face, hear those beloved words, "Well done, good and faithful servant!" (Matthew 25:23). The obedience and faithfulness of my mentors inspire me to that end.

Second, my wiser friends never cease praying for their families, friends, and neighbors. When we're wrapped up in ourselves, finding time to pray is next to impossible. Sure, we'll pray for our needs and agendas, but praying for the needs of others is rarely a priority. That's just not the case with my older, wiser friends.

They pray without ceasing (1 Thessalonians 5:17 ESV), mindful of their time so as not to waste precious moments. They go straight to the source of life. I can attest to the fact that they're praying for me because they often follow up with prayer requests I shared months prior. They care enough to ask about my life and go to battle for me in prayer. People who are self-seeking do not function this way.

I sometimes hear the critique that older people pray more because they have more free time than the rest of us. There may be a shred of truth in that critique. But I believe my older friends pray more because they've learned that life is all about Jesus. Far from having too much time on their hands, these people know how dependent every human life is on the sustainer of life. They are pleading with the one who hears, knows, and has ultimately done something about pain, grief, and suffering. They are crying out to the God who sends his Spirit upon all flesh to heal and make a way when a way doesn't seem available.

The third trait I see in my older friends, one that inspires me greatly, is a disregard for their reputation paired with a willingness to do whatever it takes to make disciples of Jesus. One of the last words Jesus spoke to his disciples is known as The Great Commission.

> *All authority in heaven and on earth has been given to me. Therefore go and make disciples of all nations, baptizing them in the name of the Father and of the Son and of the Holy Spirit, and teaching them to obey everything I have commanded you. And surely I am with you always, to the very end of the age.*
>
> *— Matthew 28:18-20*

A HEART OF HOLINESS

The wiser Christians in my life are eager to see the world transformed by the redemptive power of the gospel. For them, the words of Jesus are far more than a great Sunday school lesson; rather, they see them as marching orders—something to give their lives to. It's truly refreshing to have friends in their seventies who are willing to start new things to reach lost people with the love of Christ. They're still on mission. Retirement for them is about spending their free time sowing seeds for the kingdom of God.

Lastly, these friends seem to have a supernatural ability to laugh and cry in the same sentence. Not only do they laugh at their mistakes, but they don't take themselves too seriously. I've seen them come to tears when discussing loved ones, followed by a belly laugh moments later while reminiscing about something from the past. Their laughter, tears of joy, and lightheartedness are contagious. They're not fazed by the ups and downs of life but have their eyes fixed on the promised land ahead, where suffering and sin are no more.

I learned to keep my emotions at bay as a child. To this day, I live with an underlying stoicism, repressing any sign of emotion. Honestly, I hate it. It isn't brave, nor does it reflect the heart of God. I pray regularly that God will teach me how to cry. God has emotions. Jesus felt things deeply. One of the shortest verses in the Bible is John 11:35. Look it up. Jesus wept. He did not approach life "keeping it all together." We shouldn't either. There is space for healthy, Spirit-induced emotions.

As we continue our life's journey, our desire should be to lose more of ourselves in order to gain more of Christ—surrendering our will to the will of God. Aging well has nothing to do with our outer appearance. If we're able to maintain some of our good looks, praise God. But it's not about that. It has everything to do with the condition of our hearts.

> *The LORD does not look at the things people look at. People look at the outward appearance, but the LORD looks at the heart.*
>
> *— 1 Samuel 16:7*

Standing in awe of Jesus, even after youth and beauty flee, is the greatest sign that a person has aged well.

IN THE DAYS OF OUR YOUTH

The author of Ecclesiastes says we need to remember our Creator in *the days of our youth*. When we're young, it's easy to get distracted by the excitement of passing pleasures. It's easy to believe our body belongs to us. We believe we can do whatever we want, whenever we want, so long as we don't hurt other people. But such thinking contains a grievous error. Our bodies belong to God (1 Corinthians 6:19-20). He gave them to us to steward well, not give over to lusts or various appetites.

When we're young, death is so far from our minds that we live as if we'll never die. But life doesn't go on forever. By remembering our Creator in the days of our youth, we can have hope today and in the future. As we learn to live for him now, we'll know how to live for him then.

When I was young, I lived as if I were my own creator. I created my own path and decided what was right and wrong based on the environment around me. Looking back, my youth could've been more fruitful had I acknowledged my frailty and need for something greater than myself. I've learned that accomplishments, in and of themselves, matter very little. What counts are the things God wants to accomplish through me. The same is true for you. God wants to work through your life in powerful ways. Are you willing to let him work?

Youth is a gift. It should be received with thanksgiving, yet its ability to keep one's focus on fleeting pleasures keeps many from eternal truths. If we fixate on youth, our lives will be frustrated when our bodies begin deteriorating.

If we build our lives on anything other than Jesus, we'll be found lonely and hopeless when the days of trouble come. When we're on our deathbeds, even if someone is sitting next to us, we'll have to face that moment alone. Aside from Jesus, no one will fully understand our pain. Let's learn to remember our Creator now, so we'll remember our Creator then. He'll be present with us in a way no other person can be.

Such insights should change the way we approach the home stretch of life. It should keep us on mission. Which leads to the final aim of this chapter: encouraging older saints to press on.

THERE IS NO AGE LIMIT FOR KINGDOM WORK

I fear many older saints believe their age restricts them from redemptive work. For some, the lie that claims their time is past has triumphed in their hearts. For others, the aches and pains of aging have slowed them down enough that simple comforts are more intriguing than being part of God's redemptive mission in the world. I can't possibly know all the reasons why older Christians get off mission, but I know many do.

Our culture is obsessed with youth, and our world promotes the idea that young, beautiful people are the most valuable in society. Sadly, such thinking has made its way into the church, producing some devastating results. Lots of churches today employ young people who follow the culture rather than faithful people who follow the Creator. Our message is becoming one that resembles the heart of culture, not the heart of Christ. Something has to change.

I find myself wanting to share words of encouragement with older Christians but fear they will be taken wrongly. I don't want to sound like a young know-it-all. Despite my hesitation, the message must be heard: Older saints, your race is not finished. God has work for you to do. Although our culture values youth, God values you and is inviting you back into his redemptive work.

God has used old saints before; why wouldn't he do it again? Remember Moses? God called Moses to lead Israel out of Egypt when the prophet was eighty years old! I'm guessing at eighty, the last thing on Moses' mind was leading a dangerous rescue mission. How much strength do you think he felt in his bones? How much grit do you think he had in his heart? Likely, very little. God, however, provided Moses with all he needed to accomplish the mission. God can do the same for you. When he shows up in a burning bush and calls you to do something revolutionary, you'd be foolish to ignore him.

Moses wasn't exactly thrilled about the call. In fact, he tried to back out several times (Exodus 3:11, 13; 4:1, 10, 13). Nonetheless, God called Moses despite his age. He wasn't "too old" to carry out God's mission. I like to think his age provided an advantage because his faith muscles were more developed.

What about Abraham? He was seventy-five years old when he set off from Harran to the land God would show him (Genesis 12:4). He knew nothing about what was ahead. He was leaving all he knew behind. Would you take such a risk at seventy-five? Most people are well into retirement at that time. Yet God wasn't finished with Abram.

A HEART OF HOLINESS

Although many things are more challenging for you now than when you were young, there is still quite a bit of kingdom work that needs a laborer such as you. We already discussed some general themes in the lives of older, missional Christians. Now I want to look at three ministry-specific things I've noticed in the lives of older saints. These are things you can do regardless of your age.

Prayer

There is, perhaps, no greater calling for a Christian than prayer. It's crucial to the work of redemption. Things change when we pray. The hearts of sinners are drawn to Jesus when we pray. Heaven invades the earth when we pray. Prayer should be the serious business of every Christian. We literally talk with the Creator of the universe when we pray. How fantastic is that?

Perhaps more than anything else, prayer changes us. If we are to engage in prayer, we must come with a posture of openness, willing to let God work on the parts of our lives that need redirecting or outright chiseling. Richard Foster, in his classic work *Celebration of Discipline*, instructs,

> To pray is to change. Prayer is the central avenue God uses to transform us. If we are unwilling to change, we will abandon prayer as a noticeable characteristic of our lives. The closer we come to the heartbeat of God the more we see our need and the more we desire to be conformed to Christ.[43]

Older saints pray big prayers. They've lived long enough to realize their life is only as good as their prayer life. They can't wait to get into the presence of God. When I'm around an older, praying Christian—I mean, one who really prays—I feel a profound sense of peace. They talk with God like they believe he hears them. They make their requests from a place of faith, not wishful thinking. Their prayers are big because their God is bigger. Prayer is vital to everything.

The same can be true for you. You don't have to have a doctorate in ministry to talk with God. You don't have to acquire a special prayer language, dress a particular way, close your eyes, be ritually cleansed, or do anything else to be heard by God. Pete Greig says,

> God invites you to pray simply, directly, and truthfully in the full and wonderful weirdness of the way he's made you. Take a walk in the rain. Write prayers on the soles of your shoes. Sing the blues. Rap. Write Petrarchan sonnets. Sit in silence in a forest. Go for a run until you sense God's smile; throw yourself down a waterslide, yelling hallelujah if that's honestly your thing.[44]

Encouragement

The Bible teaches us to encourage and build one another up (1 Thessalonians 5:11). In a world where people are divided more than ever, encouragement speaks hope to others and reflects the heart of Christ. A simple word of encouragement can go a long way.

Don't be afraid to speak. Your words possess power. I've seen it over and over. I've been the recipient of such encouragement. It changes things instantly. Who doesn't need to hear a kind word? We all need it.

While in Denver, my family belonged to a small church

A HEART OF HOLINESS

led by a guy who graduated from the seminary I was attending. When I first met him, I remember feeling so loved. He was the ultimate encourager. Although I can't remember many of his sermons, I can clearly recall his smile and his ability to make me and everyone around us feel valued. His kindness was a bit of God's grace in a season that was challenging. You can be the kind of person who encourages others. It is so needed in today's world.

Friendships

One of the greatest gifts of my life has been the friendships I've made with older men. These men have led ministries, raised families, and remained committed to Jesus. Their wealth of wisdom has been a blessing to me on many occasions. I can't overstate the importance of such relationships.

Older saints must seek out younger men and women to befriend. Younger Christians who value maturity in Christ-like character will recognize the value of such relationships. If you're not in the habit of forming these relationships, it will feel awkward at first. In most cases, it's just as awkward for a young person to approach you as it is for you to approach them. We've got to get over this. Start by praying and asking God to send you a young Timothy. As you may recall, Paul mentored Timothy. God used their relationship in far-reaching ways. God can put all the pieces together for you as well.

At the very least, those are the three things you *can* do. You can pray, encourage, and make friends with Christians who are newer to the faith than you.

You must fight the excuses. Do your hips and hands hurt? Likely. Are you overlooked in ministry for younger men and women? Many times, yes. Has your energy and creativity waned? It probably feels that way. Is God finished with you? Absolutely not. He will supply you with what you're lacking. He's that kind of God.

Older saints, please press on. You have walked the path of faith longer than us newbies. And although sin continues to sway your ways and thoughts, the many victories of faith throughout your life will encourage us young wanderers.

There is nothing wrong with being young (1 Timothy 4:12), but there is nothing wrong with being old, either. God is not alarmed by your aches and pains or lack of energy. Plus, we younger Christians need you more than we let on.

Don't give up. There is no age limit for kingdom work.

CHAPTER 8

REMEMBER THAT YOU WILL DIE

Teach us to number our days, that we may gain a heart of wisdom.

—Psalm 90:12

When we were young, my brother and I spent random Sundays at our grandparents' house. These trips were magical. They lived in the country and seemed to have endless stretches of land. Their property felt like another planet. Rolling hills, pine trees, and the smell of freshly mowed grass greeted us upon every visit. We explored the terrain with all the wonder young people can conjure up.

Part of the property included beehives, which I found to be both terrifying and spectacular. I avoided them at all costs because death by a thousand bee stings sounded like a poor way to spend an afternoon. Yet I eyed them with curiosity. Raising bees was as foreign to me as the property they inhabited.

Before our visits, Grandpa carved wooden swords so we

could fight imaginary wars and conquer the surrounding lands. Those swords possessed power. They were made with love, precision, grit, and know-how. Such attributes can defeat any enemy known to humanity. I wondered if there was anything my grandpa couldn't do.

After our conquests, we'd gather around the kitchen table to experience a different kind of power—my grandma's freshly baked pies. They filled the house with the aroma of heaven. Our bellies were full, and our hearts warmed. Nothing could disturb these visits.

But good things often end without notice. Death has a way of showing up and wreaking havoc on an otherwise pleasant day. We don't think about it when we're young. It never occurred to me that visits to Grandpa's would come to an end.

> *Our days may come to seventy years, or eighty, if our strength endures; yet the best of them are but trouble and sorrow, for they quickly pass, and we fly away.*
>
> — Psalm 90:10

My grandparents flew away. No one asked me if I was okay with it. One day they were living, and the next day they weren't. Their property was sold, and their house was demolished. All that remains is my memory of it. I was utterly unprepared. I remember the shock I felt when I realized I couldn't ask my grandpa if he was okay.

UNPREPARED FOR THE INEVITABLE

Most of us are unprepared for death. I'm guessing you don't sit around talking about death with your friends and acquaintances. That would be strange. You probably don't have a death plan like an expectant mother has a birth plan. That would be even stranger. Yet avoiding the conversation isn't a good plan, either.

Life will end. We will die. Death is the great equalizer of humanity in that sense. Regardless of our earning capacity, influence, age, education level, or any other factor, death is unavoidable. No one gets out of this life alive. Timothy Keller says,

> Death is the Great Interruption, tearing loved ones away from us, or us from them. Death is the Great Schism, ripping apart the material and immaterial parts of our being and sundering a whole person, who was never meant to be disembodied, even for a moment...Death is hideous and frightening and cruel and unusual. It is not the way life is supposed to be, and our grief in the face of death acknowledges that. Death is our Great Enemy, more than anything else. It makes a claim on each and every one of us, pursuing us relentlessly through all our days.[45]

In his little book, *On Death,* Keller provides four reasons why he believes humanity is less prepared for death today than at any point in history. First, the blessing of modern medicine has hidden it from our view. Due to medical advances, it's easier than ever to dance around the inevitable. We're born in medical facilities and taken back there to die. Out of sight, out of mind. Life comes full circle in a hospital room.

Years ago, dying at home was far more common than it is today. For instance, in the nineteenth century, death was a community affair. A dying person received care in her home from her loved ones. Every household member had a front-row

A HEART OF HOLINESS

seat. Everyone contributed in some way, making it next to impossible to avoid the reality of death.

In Colonial times, the average family lost one out of three children before they reached adulthood. I can't imagine the grief of losing a child. I know parents who have walked through it. It's terrible. Furthermore, life expectancy in Colonial times was around forty years, meaning death visited homes frequently. Thankfully, advances in medicine have led to longer, healthier lives—a good gift from God worth celebrating. But we still die.

The second reason we struggle with death is because we focus on "this-world meaning and fulfillment." Because the secular viewpoint claims nothing supernatural exists, happiness is sought exclusively in things found in this life. It makes logical sense. If nothing beyond this world exists, why pretend it does? We should just carry on and have as much fun as possible. We should eat, drink, and be merry, for tomorrow we die. People who hold such a worldview have every right to feel timid when facing death and dying. It's strange, unknown, and ridiculously rude. How dare it interrupt our pursuit of happiness?

In his book, Keller shares the story of Mark Ashton, vicar of St. Andrew the Great in Cambridge, England. During Ashton's battle with gallbladder cancer, he "talked with virtually everyone he met about his coming death with ease, eloquence, and poise."[46] It won't surprise you to learn that his words were met with silence and uneasiness. Death is insulting. It's a conversation killer. Try mentioning it at a party.

The third reason we're less prepared for death than our ancestors is because many have defined it as nonexistence. When we die, we cease to exist. No heaven. No hell. The lights simply go out. Within such a framework, a deceased person has no cognitive understanding of their condition. They don't understand anything. How can they? They no longer exist here or anywhere. On one level, I understand the attractiveness of this view. If I could live how I wanted without ever facing a God who confronts my behavior, I'd certainly be tempted to do so. Yet if such a worldview is true, life has no ultimate meaning.

William Lane Craig states it well:

> If each individual person passes out of existence when he dies, then what ultimate meaning can be given to his life? Does it really matter in the end whether he ever existed at all? Sure, his life may be important relative to certain other events, but what's the ultimate significance of any of those events? If everything is doomed to destruction, then what does it matter that you influenced anything? Ultimately it makes no difference.[47]

The key word is *ultimately*. In a thousand years, does it really matter that we got a promotion, made money, or became an influencer? How can any achievement have significance in the grand scheme of things? They can't if nothing beyond this life exists.

Lastly, we struggle with death because we've lost categories for sin, guilt, and forgiveness. Those words once provided clarity and a path forward to the sense of morality found in every human heart. We do our best to ignore them today. We don't like feeling bad about our decisions. We don't like the difficult work of forgiveness, so we avoid it. Friedrich Nietzsche is famous, in part, for his argument that humanity's feelings of indebtedness stem from people's belief in God. Indeed, many thinkers argue that once people eradicate their belief in a God of judgment, the burdensome feelings of guilt and shame will disappear with it. Religion is to blame for our woes, according

A HEART OF HOLINESS

to such logic, and doing away with it is the surest way to attain happiness and freedom.

The world is vastly secular today. Belief in a God of judgment has been replaced by belief in a God who's never angry about anything, or, in many cases, belief in no God at all. Yet people still have moral reflexes they can neither ignore nor destroy. Thankfully, there's a remedy for our guilt and fear of death, and it doesn't involve wishful thinking or doing away with religion. It involves Jesus, who cares for us, loves us, and has done something about our indebtedness.

According to Keller, Christianity is different from other religions.

> It doesn't leave you to face death on your own, by holding up your life record and hoping it will suffice. Instead it gives you a champion who has defeated death, who pardons you and covers you with his love. You face death 'in him' and with his perfect record (Philippians 3:9). To the degree we believe, know, and embrace that, we are released from the power of death.[48]

Death is never pleasant. It's an intruder, an enemy opposed to God's will. Nevertheless, we don't have to be unprepared for life's inevitable end. When we're faced with it, whether through the loss of a loved one or in the midst of our own dying, recalling Jesus' victory over death on our behalf, which he accomplished by rising from the grave, should encourage our hearts and prepare our minds. All who believe in Jesus will live, even though they die. And whoever lives by believing in him will never die (John 11:25-26). Do you believe this?

THE ABSURDITY OF SELFISHNESS AND THE CERTAINTY OF DEATH

I recently read *When Breath Becomes Air* by Paul Kalanithi. Kalanithi was a young neurosurgeon who developed stage four lung cancer and documented his dying days in a book.[49] He led a life of promise and potential. He would have been a successful doctor, no doubt. Everything was going well for him. He experienced great success in his educational pursuits. He had a loving wife, a baby daughter, and a budding medical career. Then cancer entered his story and changed everything about it.

Around the same time I was reading his memoir, I found a story online about a girl named Brooklyn who, like Kalanithi, was dying of cancer and writing about her journey. Both accounts gave me a profound sense that, because death is certain, selfishness is absurd. In one post, written from her hospital room, Brooklyn said,

> I'm here to tell you not to waste your time binging Netflix, marathoning YouTube, or scrolling through social media. I'm here to tell you that, as a Christian, our constant consideration should be, "If Jesus was sitting here next to me, would He approve of what I'm doing?"[50]

It's a powerful question every Christian should ask themselves. How are we spending our time? Are our pursuits honoring God?

Stories like Brooklyn's confront us with the truth that life is more than our selfish desires, goals, and dreams. None of our pursuits, apart from Christ, amount to anything in the end. Death is certain. It's coming for us all, and in light of it, selfishness is absurd.

A HEART OF HOLINESS

Everything we own belongs to future garage sales and landfills. The home we renovate and modernize will go out of style and be sold to someone who will replace the flooring, paint, and cabinets with something more desirable to them. Our hard work will amount to nothing in the end. Admiration for a job well done will not continue into retirement. Someone else will take our job and do it better than we did. All the achievements from our careers will be forgotten when we die. Even our first names will be unknown to our great-grandchildren.[51] They'll have little to no knowledge of our story. Honestly, when we live for anything other than Christ, death is the ultimate slap in the face. Nothing we do will outlast the grave. Death is final.

Why, then, do we live in a self-saturated world? We all see it. We all experience it. Death is not slowing us down or redirecting our steps. When we watch television, scroll social media, navigate the airport, or shop at grocery stores, we witness the reality of self-centeredness and how it pollutes everything and everyone. Even though selfishness is an undesirable trait in people, one we notice in others yet manage to overlook in ourselves, many spend their lives perfecting it like a trade. We are anxious, stressed out, and exhausted by our pursuit of self. Is there a better way?

The dying have much to teach us about living, for when their dreams vanish in the midst of death, their perspective often shifts from themselves to others—a place where wisdom thrives. At the close of his book, Kalanithi acknowledged the joy others bring to our existence. Far from boasting about his educational accolades or anything else he accomplished in life, he turned his attention to his eight-month-old daughter. Realizing her age prevented her from carrying any memory of him into the future, he spoke some heartfelt words:

When you come to one of the many moments in life where you must give an account of yourself, provide a ledger of what you have been, and done, and meant to the world, do not, I pray, discount that you filled a dying man's days with a sated joy, a joy unknown to me in all my prior years, a joy that does not hunger for more and more but rests, satisfied. In this time, right now, that is an enormous thing.[52]

A PECULIAR KIND OF WISDOM

It's easy to live with a skewed sense of time. From gym memberships and plastic surgery to youth obsessions and dietary fads, we fight against our mortality. According to Psalm 90:12, wisdom is found when we acknowledge the brevity of life. It's a peculiar kind of wisdom, no doubt, but the implication is clear: Numbering our days leads to wisdom.

To number our days means to acknowledge that our time on earth is limited. We will not live forever. We have an expiration date. Instead of recognizing the shortness of life and letting it inform our days, we often behave as if ample time were before us—time for exploring our dreams, expressing ourselves, and seeking pleasures forevermore. In essence, we become me-centric. Our motives scream, "Me first. My happiness. My goals and dreams. My desires. My life." Our decisions are made without any real reference to God, eternity, or others. We may pay lip service to them, but the motives of our hearts are concerned with gratifying the desires of the flesh (Galatians 5:16). Let me suggest five ways we can grow in wisdom by numbering our days.

First, numbering our days helps us grow in humility. We didn't ask to come to earth, and we don't have the ability to stay. Our life is a mist that appears for a little while then vanishes (James 4:14). Life is not about us. We are created beings. Created on purpose for a purpose. Our lives only make sense in reference to the One who created them. If we lose sight of him, we grow in pride, not humility.

> Humility is simply the disposition that prepares the soul for living in trust.[53]
>
> — Andrew Murray

Are we trusting in God or self? Is our life marked by the crucified Christ or by self-seeking, self-will, self-confidence, and self-exaltation? Our inevitable deaths should create in us a heart of humility. It's foolish to think life is about us.

Second, numbering our days will help us prioritize what matters most. Consider how you spend your time. Are you investing in people and sowing seeds for God's kingdom, or are you exhaustively trying to prove yourself to others? Are you identifying people who need to get in the game and helping them walk in holiness, or are you developing your own spiritual rhythms without any regard for the needs of others?

Our lives are not our own. We were bought with a price—the precious blood of Christ (1 Corinthians 6:19-20). He's the one who came to serve, not to be served (Mark 10:45). He's the good shepherd who laid his life down for the sheep (John 10:11). When we follow him without regard for our own lives, he directs our steps and keeps us from fruitless endeavors. He protects his flock from wolves. He guides us toward that which is beautiful and holy, magnificent and God-glorifying. The people in our lives matter more than the things in them. Our work has eternal significance. Our days are spent prioritizing what matters most.

Third, numbering our days produces gratitude in our hearts

for life's simple pleasures. Joy exists in this world. For me, sunsets, a good cup of coffee, mountain vacations, friendships, a fantasy novel, and bicycle rides bring a smile to my face. We engage in these things differently, however, depending on our beliefs about life. If we believe this life is all there is and nothing afterwards, our affections attach to things made in a store, as it were. When the true nature of worldliness is revealed, whether through death or dying, our joy is pulled from under us, and we become discouraged, or worse, depressed. Apart from Christ, life as we know it loses its appeal. Everything we believe about the world becomes disordered. We feel disoriented and confused. In many cases, we grow angry and distance ourselves from the people closest to us.

It's a little ironic, really. Because we assume our days will last forever, life's simple pleasures are taken for granted, such as walking, breathing, hearing, seeing, working, dreaming, creativity, and traveling with ease. Life is all around us, but we miss it because we don't realize how fleeting it is. Life's pleasures are not guaranteed (just ask your grandparents), but they certainly feel like they are when we're young.

Fourth, numbering our days helps us store up treasure in heaven. Jesus was a masterful teacher. The best teacher to ever live. During his famous sermon on the mount, he shared these words with his followers:

> *Don't store up for yourselves treasures on earth, where moth and rust destroy and where thieves break in and steal. But store up for yourselves treasures in heaven, where neither moth nor rust destroys, and where thieves don't break in and steal. For where your treasure is, there your heart will be also.*
>
> *— Matthew 6:19-21 CSB*

A HEART OF HOLINESS

Jesus is not just sharing good advice. He's teaching his followers a very important lesson: Our attention is given to the things we value most. If our treasure is found in this world, we'll miss out on what Jesus wants to do most in us and through us, namely, make us like himself—people who walk in humility, grace, and, ultimately, holiness forever. If our hobbies are most important to us, worshiping with God's people on Sunday morning will take a back seat. If binge-watching the latest season of our favorite show is most important to us, spending time in God's Word will fall to the wayside.[54]

Lastly, numbering our days helps us worship the one who defeated death. Jesus is worthy of our adoration for many wonderful, awe-inspiring reasons, not least of which is his conquering of death, by which we too, in our eventual deaths, find life through resurrection. Such life is given to anyone who places faith in Jesus. Words cannot express how marvelous this truth is. We can and must worship Jesus because he paid it all.

Yes, though it may be unusual considering the world and its ways, learning to number our days will produce in us a heart of holiness. We will grow in humility, have better priorities, enjoy more of life's simple pleasures, store up treasure in heaven, and worship in ways fitting for a redeemed child of God.

MEMENTO MORI

Reminders are helpful. Many of us need them to function like responsible adults. For me, setting a reminder on my phone helps me get my recycling to the curb for pickup on Tuesday mornings and my trash on Fridays. Without the reminder, I'd forget every week. I've learned the trash man comes by our neighborhood once, whether my can is sitting in the driveway or not. It would be great if he'd stop and knock on my door, kindly reminding me of trash day. But he doesn't do that. So, I need a reminder.

Death is similar. We need reminders. Because the world does a great job of hiding it from us, we need rhythms in our lives that keep the reality of death before us.

Memento mori is a Latin phrase meaning "remember that you will die." The concept is often seen in art visuals today, such as skulls, skeletons, and hourglasses. I know people who have these themes tattooed on them as a reminder of their mortality. In Puritan New England, it was common to worship at churches with elaborate tombstones stretching across the landscape. The interior design of these spaces was simple, but the graveyards upon entering were a bit jarring, producing a death-awareness in everyone entering for worship.[55] The leaders of these churches wanted to remind their people that life is short. They didn't want them to waste time on trivial pursuits. I hope this chapter has been for you a little like those gravesites were for them—a helpful, though sobering, reminder that you will die.

If you haven't experienced the death of someone close to you, it's only a matter of time. As we age, such occurrences become common. A lot of death exists in our future. Although it's tempting to avoid deathbeds, funerals, memorials, and other events that come with death and dying, much is gained by stepping into these moments. Let me share two reasons why engaging death in all its various stages is a good plan.

First, when we have conversations with the dying, especially those we know and love, important matters can rise to the surface that have, in many cases, laid dormant for a lifetime. There's often vulnerability and honesty among people facing imminent death. It's not guaranteed, so we have to be sensitive to the moment, but it's fascinating what people will share when counting down the days.

A HEART OF HOLINESS

Second, God created us to be a blessing to others. As we've discussed at various places throughout this book, life is not about us. When armed with that truth, we can do some positive things for the dying and the loved ones of the deceased. For instance, when we enter the room of a dying person, our presence can bring comfort. A simple smile and a hello go further than we think.

Imagine approaching death alone. Nobody should have to do that. When we enter the room of a dying person, our presence is welcomed. If we can pray with them, that's even better. Our prayers can remind them of God's presence, care, and love. Don't underestimate the power of presence while with a dying person.

The same is true for our presence with those grieving the loss of a loved one. What a great opportunity funerals and memorials offer to bring the comfort of God to mourning people. The ministry of presence, which is simply spending time with others in a physical space, can shower the grieving with a tangible expression of love. Don't worry about words. We don't have to know all the right things to say. It's generally better to say very little in these moments, anyway. Listening and being present can speak volumes to a grieving person.

As we conclude this chapter, it's wise to turn our attention to Psalm 39. Death is bewildering. So is dying. King David knew that emotion well. He penned the following words. Let's treat them as a prayer.

> *Show me, LORD, my life's end and the number of my days; let me know how fleeting my life is.*
>
> *— Psalm 39:4*

EPILOGUE

PURSUING HOLINESS IN AN UNHOLY WORLD

*For God did not call us to be impure,
but to live a holy life.*

—1 Thessalonians 4:7

Throughout the centuries, Christians have faced the difficult task of pursuing holiness in an unholy world. Since the fall of humanity, recorded in the third chapter of Genesis, people have invented ways of doing evil (Romans 1:30), making holy living difficult for God's redeemed people. Obeying God's Word exposes us to ridicule and division.

Yet God is holy and seeks a holy people (1 Peter 1:16). Our pursuit of holiness can't be an afterthought, like adding an ingredient to a soup at the last minute. We must develop new rhythms and fresh perspectives, which are actually old rhythms and biblical perspectives. In many cases, we must swim against the tide of culture.

A Christian's moral standard is determined by Scripture alone, not laws or cultural whims. When a nation's laws violate clear commands of Scripture, Christians must oppose them for the sake of holiness and obedience to God. When people's fancies rule the day, God's Word must rule the hearts of his people instead.

Being set apart in an unholy world will prove challenging as the world journeys further away from the biblical understanding of wholeness and human flourishing. Recently, a friend shared a research poll with me about how Americans have pulled back from values that once defined them.[56] The poll looked at the shift in these values from 1998 to 2023. The values were patriotism, religion, having children, community involvement, and money. It shocked me to see that every value except money decreased by at least 20%. Patriotism was down 32%; religion was down 23%; having children was down 29%; and community involvement was down 20%. We don't need expertise to recognize that individualism is on the rise.

All the values listed necessitate other people, except money. Community can't happen alone. Nor can we have children alone. Even patriotism and religion require other people, whether through celebratory events or religious gatherings. But money—now that's a whole different matter. We can pursue money on our own and for our own gain. All we have to do is be better than our opponents, smarter than our competitors, and wiser than our neighbors. Pursuing money is a game every person plays for themselves. It's about eliminating others, not including them.

The Bible says, "Where you have envy and selfish ambition, there you find disorder and every evil practice" (James 3:16). Selfishness mixed with envy breeds disorder. Should that surprise us? When our media outlets tell us about wars, scandals, racial injustice, school shootings, sex trafficking, and various infringements, we're simply seeing the outcropping of envy and selfish ambition. The Bible doesn't say *some* evil practices stem from these things, but rather, *every* evil practice. In other words, all the evil in the world has roots in these two vices.

To avoid being polluted by the world, as the book of James alludes to (James 1:27), we must take drastic measures. Think of Christ's words about tearing out an eye or cutting off a hand or foot if they cause us to sin (Matthew 18:8-9). I don't think Jesus wants us to mutilate ourselves, but I do think he wants us to take sin seriously. If we binge-watch shows with questionable content, it might mean getting rid of our devices. If we fall into a comparison trap while scrolling through social media, it might mean deleting our accounts. If our smartphones entice us to visit pornographic websites, it might mean replacing them with dumbphones.

I understand all this talk about holiness sounds negative and obsessive. Yet the influence of unholiness is like wildfire. If we want to avoid being burned, we have to play both offense and defense. Our chances of victory decrease if our play is one-sided.

I pray this book hasn't laid an unnecessary burden on you. There are enough books like those in the world. I wanted to help people walk in freedom and wholeness. Perhaps the best way to accomplish that is by listening to and applying the Word of God.

God's Word is a lamp to the feet—a light to the path of those who obey it (Psalms 119:105).

> *For the word of God is living and effective and sharper than any double-edged sword, penetrating as far as the separation of soul and spirit, joints and marrow. It is able to judge the thoughts and intentions of the heart.*

—Hebrews 4:12 CSB

A HEART OF HOLINESS

God's Word will not lead us astray. It will make us wise and create in us a heart like his. We should read it often and not give up.

ACKNOWLEDGEMENTS

I am grateful for the many people who provided feedback, encouragement, and help during the writing of this book. It wouldn't be what it is without their contributions. Of course, all errors, theological or otherwise, are mine.

I'd like to thank my wife, Rachel. Not only did she provide editorial suggestions, but she endured countless hours of me living in my head as I attempted to flesh out this book at the most inconvenient times. Thank you for bearing with me. You have a front-row seat to my life. Any holiness I've attained is largely because of your support and willingness to help me see my blind spots.

I'm also indebted to the following people: Leland Woelk, who worked through the entire manuscript and provided a notebook of feedback; Bob Tlapek, who read the majority of the early manuscript and provided thoughts along the way; Ron Watts and Benjamin Vrbicek, who provided content feedback and wrote endorsements; Drew Wilson, who checked the accuracy of all Scripture references; and Brett Cheek, who provided feedback for two chapters and challenged me to write each day, speeding up the completion of this book. I appreciate each one of you.

Patricia Kuper edited the book during the first half of December 2023. Your work taught me a great deal about writing, and your kind words about the final product made me smile.

I'd like to thank Alex Hicks, who, during our meetings over coffee, encouraged me to see the project through. Something about our Nashville trip fueled the fire; maybe it was the caffeine.

Collin Smith created the artwork and laid out the text for print and electronic distribution. Thanks for being flexible and helping me publish my first book.

Matt Lynn, Joe Class, and Ola Nordstrom showed interest in the project and encouraged me in various ways. Your timely words kept me going when I felt like quitting.

ENDNOTES

INTRODUCTION

1   This language comes from William Ernest Henley's poem, *Invictus*.

2   As best I can tell, seeing God means perceiving his activities in our lives and world. Sin blinds us to his presence, but holiness reveals it in wonderful, life-giving ways.

3   N. T. Wright makes this argument in his book, *Scripture and the Authority of God* (HarperCollins, 2011), 21.

4   Kevin DeYoung, *The Hole in Our Holiness* (Crossway, 2012), 31.

5   There's a great chapter on this topic in Peter Scazzero's book, *Emotionally Healthy Discipleship* (Zondervan, 2021).

6   It would be helpful to have a Bible handy as you read this book so you can look up biblical references as they appear.

7   I'll merely scratch the surface of this topic here. To explore it further, check out John Mark Comer's excellent book, *Live No Lies: Recognize and Resist the Three Enemies That Sabotage Your Peace*, (WaterBrook, 2021).

8   It can mean more than this, but the definition given here, from John Stott's commentary, *The Letters of John: An Introduction and Commentary* (IVP Academic, 2009), 102, is the primary focus in this context. See chapter 4 for a more detailed

discussion.

9   C. S. Lewis, *The Screwtape Letters* (HarperCollins, 2001).

CHAPTER ONE

10   To see how you compare financially to the rest of the world, visit howrichami.givingwhatwecan.org.

11   Timothy Keller, *Counterfeit Gods: The Empty Promises of Money, Sex, and Power, and the Only Hope That Matters* (Dutton, 2009), 52.

CHAPTER TWO

12   God created people with amazing gifts and abilities. We should celebrate good work and creativity as much as possible. The Bible and all of human history end with God making a city where he's king. Check out Revelation 21 and 22. The point I'm making here is that a city plus God's presence is "good"; a city plus human ego is "evil."

13   Richard S. Hess, *The Old Testament: A Historical, Theological, and Critical Introduction* (Baker Academic, 2016), 27.

14   Mental health and depression are complex topics far beyond the scope of this book. Social media isn't to blame for all of it, but I believe it plays a role.

15   Lots of people find an identity in what they don't have or in the suffering they're experiencing. It works both ways.

16   In chapter 4, we'll discuss the rationale for this suggestion in more detail.

CHAPTER THREE

17   C. S. Lewis, *Mere Christianity* (HarperCollins, 1980), 128.

18   See Luke 15:11-32.

19   Quoted in Peter Scazzero's book, *Emotionally Healthy Relationships Day by Day* (Zondervan, 2017), 31.

20   Nancy R. Pearcy, *Love Thy Body: Answering Hard Questions about Life and Sexuality* (Baker Books, 2018), 27.

CHAPTER FOUR

21   Marianne Meye Thompson, *The IVP New Testament Commentary Series: 1-3 John* (InterVarsity Press, 1992), 68.
22   Stott, *The Letters of John*, 102.
23   Timothy Keller, *Galatians for You* (The Good Book Company, 2013), 17.
24   Richard Foster, *Celebration of Discipline*, (HarperOne, 2018), 84.
25   See Craig Blomberg, *Neither Poverty nor Riches* (Eerdmans, 1999).
26   John Mark Comer, *The Ruthless Elimination of Hurry* (Waterbrook, 2019), 172.

CHAPTER FIVE

27   John Mark Comer, *Practicing the Way: Be with Jesus. Become like him. Do as he did.* (Waterbrook, 2024).
28   Lewis, *Mere Christianity*, 226.
29   Prayer is also important for following Jesus. We must talk with him regularly, which, in its essence, is what prayer is. Here, however, we'll stick with Scripture and the local church.
30   Denver Seminary has a great bibliography online. They update it regularly. Everything listed comes from a broadly evangelical viewpoint; that is, all the resources were produced by men and women who believe in the divine inspiration and inerrancy of Scripture. Search "Denver Seminary Bibliography" online to find it.
31   For help with scripture memorization, check out Glenna Marshall, *Memorizing Scripture: The Basics, Blessings, and Benefits of Meditating on God's Word* (Moody Publishers, 2023).

32 J. T. English, *Deep Discipleship* (B&H Publishing, 2020), 83.

CHAPTER SIX

33 Parts of this section was first published at https://servantsofgrace.org/humanitys-greatest-problem-and-the-hope-of-christ/. It was written during the beginning of the coronavirus pandemic in 2020.

34 We'll primarily look at sin here. Death will be the topic of Chapter 8.

35 I'd encourage you to check out Jerry Bridges' thoughts on this point in his book, *The Discipline of Grace* (NavPress, 2006), 36.

36 Ibid., 51.

37 Keller, *Galatians for You*, 10.

38 If you want to learn more about Christ's heart for you in your worst moments, read Dane Ortlund's fantastic book, *Gentle and Lowly* (Crossway, 2020). You won't be disappointed.

39 Bridges, *The Discipline of Grace*, 44.

40 I never want to put someone's pain in print, especially when they've entrusted me with it. Therefore, the story told in this section has been changed to protect confidentiality, but it's based on true events.

41 https://iowasheep.com/wp-content/uploads/2018/09/follow_the_leader-1.pdf. Accessed on June 29, 2023.

CHAPTER SEVEN

42 https://www.businessinsider.com/beauty-multibillion-industry-trends-future-2019-7#:~:text=The%20beauty%20industry%20is%20growing,from%20retail%20analytics%20firm%20Edited. Accessed on May 17, 2023.

43 Foster, *Celebration of Discipline*, 33.

44   Pete Greig, *How to Pray: A Simple Guide for Normal People* (NavPress, 2019), 18.

CHAPTER EIGHT

45   Timothy Keller, *On Death* (Penguin Books, 2020), 1.

46   Ibid., 12.

47   William Lane Craig, *On Guard: Defending Your Faith with Reason and Precision* (David C. Cook, 2010), 32.

48   Keller, *On Death*, 31.

49   Paul Kalanithi, *When Breath Becomes Air* (Random House, 2016).

50   https://fightoffaithblog.com/2022/02/24/dying-young-woman-has-a-message-for-us/. Accessed on September 29, 2023.

51   Sam Allberry, *James for You* (The Good Book Company, 2015), 122.

52   Kalanithi, *When Breath Becomes Air*, 199.

53   Andrew Murray, *Humility: The Journey Toward Holiness* (Bethany House, 2001), 78.

54   On the other hand, if we cultivate habits of holiness, our hobbies turn toward him. Reading the Bible, praying, listening to worship music, or giving of our time and resources are all wonderful hobbies.

55   https://www.thegospelcoalition.org/article/memento-mori/?amp. Accessed May 12, 2023.

EPILOGUE

56   https://www.instagram.com/p/CqS-X_LM-wA6/?igshid=MDJmNzVkMjY%3D. Accessed March 29, 2023.

Made in the USA
Columbia, SC
19 August 2024